THE
Catholic Wedding
BOOK

REVISED EDITION

A Complete Guidebook
for brides, grooms, and their parents,
with instructions for planning the ritual,
managing people and details in the best possible style,
and keeping a sense of humor when everyone else
is panicking.

Molly K. Hans and William C. Graham

PAULIST PRESS
New York/Mahwah, NJ

Cover and book design by Lynn Else
Illustrations by Christopher Fay

Text copyright © 2007 by Molly K. Hans and William C. Graham

Library of Congress Cataloging-in-Publication Data

Hans, Molly K., 1953–
    The Catholic wedding book : a complete guidebook for brides, grooms, and their parents, with instructions for planning the ritual, managing people, and details in the best possible style, and keeping a sense of humor when everyone else is panicking / Molly K. Hans and William C. Graham.—Rev. ed.
        p. cm.
    ISBN 978-0-8091-4462-4 (alk. paper)
    1. Marriage service. 2. Weddings. 3. Catholic Church—Liturgy. I. Graham, William C., 1950– II. Title.
BX2250.S74 2007
264′.02085—dc22

                                                          2007006254

Published by Paulist Press
997 Macarthur Boulevard
Mahwah, New Jersey 07430

www.paulistpress.com

Printed and bound in the United States of America

Dedicated

to the memory of
Paul Francis Anderson,
the fifth bishop of Duluth,
who loved and taught his people well.

Acknowledgments

We are grateful to
the brides and grooms, their mothers and fathers,
our priest friends and associates,
and our families and friends
who have challenged us
to grow in patience,
in wisdom,
and in holiness.

What has been is what will be,
  and what has been done is what will be done;
and there is nothing new under the sun.
                    —Ecclesiastes 1:9

And he who sat upon the throne said,
  "Behold, I make all things new."
                    —Revelation 21:5

A Wedding Prayer

God of all grace, giver of all gifts,
you have given us the sacrament of marriage
so that man and woman might live together in love
and be for us a sign of your far greater and perfecting love.
Hear our prayer today
for those who enter marriage:
make them healthy and happy and holy
all the days of their lives,
both today and forever
with Jesus, our Christ and our brother.

Amen!

A Wedding Blessing

May the Lord who lives in light come near your lives
with the undying brilliance of radiant love.

May the One who does not diminish
as shadows bring the night
protect you under his eagle wing.

May he give you the strength to be gentle
and the will to be kind,
making holy the moments and the years of your love,
enriching you always with family and with friends.

May your hearts be open to the Word
and, at last, when you come to rest,
may you know unending peace
in the Father, the Son, and the Holy Spirit. Amen!

(Adapted from John R. Roach's blessing over the city of
St. Paul at his installation as archbishop)

A Letter

Dear Bride and Groom,

The time has come, the Walrus said, to talk of many things. There are indeed many things to talk over as you prepare to exchange your vows within a Catholic ceremony. Whether you plan to be surrounded by a few close friends and family members or as many guests as the fire marshal will allow, there are important decisions to be made. The details can be so numerous that they threaten to over-shadow the importance of the occasion. Often you might wish for the flick of a magic wand that will bring "happily ever after" to instant reality.

During these festive months of preparation for your wedding day and married life, seek to examine both who you are and who you hope to become. Look closely at what you are about. Try to understand both the nuances and the impact of the preparation for and celebration of your wedding. Let your prayerful preparation be a model for the life you are beginning together.

Our fond hope is that this book will help you as you think of these many things, and that it will assist you in celebrating your wedding with confidence—and fun!

May the gracious God who has begun this good work in you carry it through to completion.

The Authors

Contents

Part II: Behind the Scenes

Part III: Beyond the Footlights

PART I
Getting Your Act Together

THE CAST

The Bride and Groom

Uncle Woody and Aunt Janice receive a Christmas card from their favorite niece, Cara. As far as the new year is concerned, Cara has only one thing on her mind. "The wedding is three months away," she writes. "Now the pressure is really on!"

Uncle Woody, the father of four boys, shakes his head and mutters, "Pressure? How much pressure can there be when the wedding is still three months away?" Aunt Janice wisely keeps her thoughts to herself.

Do you have extra closet or drawer space? Of course not. We use up as much space as we have. The same with time. Your engagement, whatever its length, will be filled with details large and small. There are so many things to do and worry about that it often seems there isn't enough time or energy to prepare adequately for both a wedding and a marriage. However, there are many aspects of putting together this biggest day of your life that prove to be good training for the 'Til Death Do Us Part marathon.

SETTING PRIORITIES

Once your love deepens to the point where you finally decide to commit marriage, you will begin to collect lists. It's unavoidable. They will come at you from a dizzying variety of sources: bridal magazines, etiquette books, the church, your mother, your partner, your partner's mother, your mother's partner, the photographer, the photographer's partner, your cousin Lisa or Bart who attended Catholic school for a year and could have written this book, and on and on and on.

All of these lists will include either *should* or *must*. This is because the author is convinced that what she or he is suggesting is more important than anything else that anyone else will suggest to you.

A single person has little trouble dealing with the endless "to-do" list. Acting alone, you are free to say yes or no and live with the consequences. As half of a married couple, you will consider the needs, resources, and schedule of another person in making decisions that affect both of you.

Newlyweds are easy targets for shrewd salespeople who rely on the fact that each of you is unsure how the other really feels about the necessity of the product. Suddenly both partners are signing a contract for a big-ticket item that neither wanted. When you were single, you would have told the salesperson immediately what he could do with all twenty-two volumes of *The Encyclopedia of Cuban Baseball*. When you are married a few years, you will know whether your spouse considers it a worthwhile investment. But now it's a problem. During an engagement you have ample opportunity to exercise your aptitude for making joint decisions about all kinds of things, from the best place for a honeymoon to the size and location of an apartment. You will learn which decisions need consultation and which do not. The groom may not care what font is used on the invitations. But if the groom is a printer or a commercial artist, the wise bride learns that these things might be important to him. When the groom gets junk mail from every resort in the northern hemisphere, he should ask the bride whether she wants to see it before it goes into the circular file. During your engagement you will receive invitations from local businesses, civic organizations, and the adult friends of your parents. These invitations should not be accepted or refused by either of you until the other has been consulted.

Preparing for a wedding is a good time to have discussions that center on "This is important, or unimportant, for me. Now, what is important for us?"

DIVISION OF LABOR

A visitor from Mars observing what goes on in planning a modern American wedding would logically assume that two women from the same family are getting married— a mother and her daughter.

In many weddings, the men are allowed to get away with "Just tell me where and when you want me and I'll be there."

Brides who are willing to relieve grooms of all the picky details involved in a wedding may find themselves forever responsible for all the picky details involved in the celebration of the major holidays as well as christenings, graduations, birthdays, housewarmings, and Super Bowl Sundays.

Brides who cheerfully write all the thank-you notes for both sides of the family will be expected to do Christmas cards every year just as cheerfully. The groom who shops for insurance or a mortgage all by himself teaches his partner nothing more useful than where to find the dotted line.

Maybe you enjoy talking to the photographer and the florist and the caterer, and your intended does not. Maybe you like doing income tax returns and your intended does not. If it seems more efficient to tackle these jobs alone, then maybe it is more efficient. But when you hear yourself muttering, "I sure could use some help around here," stop muttering and start communicating with your partner. If you have asked for help in the process, you will be able to rejoice together in the success of the product.

COMPROMISE

Engaged couples quickly discover that *compromise* is a word married couples use when they really mean "giving in." Compromise is the foundation of those mythical fifty-fifty marriages. Has anyone ever known of a fifty-fifty relationship that lasted longer than twenty minutes? A fifty-fifty relationship is the one you have with a cab driver—you agree to pay the fare in return for a ride to your destination.

Compromise conjures images of two kindergartners trading lollipops. I'll give you a Citrus Punch and a Yabba Dabba Dewberry for three Cha Cha Cherries. Actually it's more like a birthday party. I'll give you what you need and want whether I get anything from you or not. This is expressed in the vows. Each of you promises to be true in good times and bad, to love and honor all the days of your life. Nowhere does the word *if* appear in the vows.

There are many situations in which a compromise is simply impossible. When the groom wants a marching band to play at the wedding and the bride wants a string quartet, they will not be able to agree on a middle ground because there is none that will satisfy both negotiators. Later, when she wants a condo in Los Angeles and he wants a two-story Colonial in Baltimore, a rambler in Buzzard Lips, Wyoming, will not be a compromise.

Engaged couples soon realize that compromise really means taking turns giving in cheerfully and gracefully. The challenge lies in making adjustments when one partner is giving in more often than the other. So when you hear yourselves arguing about whether to have the wedding at 11:00 or 11:30, don't end it with "Let's not fight about this." Go ahead and fight about it. It will be good practice for later on, when one of you argues that Christmas just isn't Christmas without a real Christmas tree, and the other contends that an artificial one is cheaper and more practical. Or one insists that the children take piano lessons and the other always hated piano lessons. Or one wants to spend the income tax return on a home theater system and the other wants to remodel the bathroom. Decisions about career changes and family planning pale in comparison to the intensity and frequency of these other domestic discussions.

AMAZING SOCIAL GRACES

It's only a matter of time after the wedding when it will happen. The phone will ring, and the new bride will answer and be asked whether Mrs. Miniver is in. She will instruct the caller that a wrong number has been reached, give the interested party her mother-in-law's number, and hang up. The new groom will attend the office party and introduce his lovely date as his wife, but somehow *wife* sounds funny when he says it out loud.

By the simple act of taking a spouse, you are entering a new segment of society. You will not look different and you may not feel different, but as married people you will be treated differently.

Throughout your teen years, your mother considered you incapable of handling any task more complicated than answering the phone. Your father asked every spring if you remembered to get tags for your car. Whenever you acted half-human, your parents' friends would cluck appreciatively and murmur, "Such a nice boy." Now they will expect some very adult behavior to go along with your new lifestyle. The engagement period is a good time to sharpen some of the social skills your parents have tried to convince you were necessary, because now they are.

For instance, your parents are probably more than willing to help you plan the wedding, but they are just as busy during the day as you are. There is no reason that they should have to make phone calls, reservations, and appointments for you.

Between now and the wedding, you will be showered often with gifts, invitations, compliments, and advice. If you learn to be gracious in your acceptance and quick with your thanks while you are engaged, it will become second nature by the time you are married.

When you were single, you may have been slow to introduce yourself to others at social or business gatherings. When alone, a shy person may act invisible. But when your spouse is by your side, you may not consign her or him to the same fate. Whenever you encounter a friend or relative who does not know your partner, introductions are mandatory. A spouse who is not introduced promptly might understand that you are shy, that this is difficult for you, and that you don't intend to cause hurt feelings. But you would do well to cultivate the thoughtful habit of demonstrating your love for your partner by proudly introducing him or her to all your friends.

There are lots of interesting rules and helpful hints for developing all sorts of social skills. The etiquette book sitting right next to your Bible covers many other details besides who stands where in the receiving line. Read on. There are helpful guidelines for how to issue and respond to invitations, write thank-you notes, announce births, and correspond with the president (one never knows). Becoming familiar with correct procedures makes life easier, believe it or not, and frees you from worrying about the best way to go about being polite.

Formal announcement of your decision to marry engages you in any number of activities, some of which you may not have anticipated. Be attentive to these new demands and you'll get off to a great start.

Catholics Who Marry Other Christians or Non-Christians

Some years ago, it was presumed that Catholics married other Catholics. Any deviation from this practice was called a "mixed marriage" and was met with considerable lack of enthusiasm. Progress has been made since the days when a Catholic marrying anyone other than another Catholic was given but two options: Exchange vows in the priest's study, or live in sin.

It is not uncommon for two Christians of different denominations to enter marriage together. If the wedding is in a Catholic church, most priests are quite good about welcoming the participation of another minister. Some will invite the visitor to say a prayer, pronounce a blessing, read from scripture, or preach the homily. Much will depend on what is customary among local churches.

Tip Tap

Thump Thump

When a Catholic marries someone who is not Christian, the approach calls for both frankness and delicacy. Religious differences here are certainly more pronounced than between Lutherans and Catholics. To begin with, it is understandable that a Jew might not want his or her marriage to a Catholic blessed "in the name of the Father, and of the Son, and of the Holy Spirit."

Many rabbis will not take part in a wedding uniting a Jew and a Gentile. Before you call the caterer, call both the priest and rabbi, ask for an appointment, and see what the customs and traditions are in your area.

Some bishops will permit a wedding of this sort to take place in a hotel ballroom or at another secular site; others will not. Ask your priest how this situation has been approached before. (See the Dispensation Form in part II.)

Whenever he or she marries someone who isn't Catholic, the Catholic party is asked "to do all I can to share the faith I have received with our children by having them baptized and educated as Catholics." Some who prepare for marriage find this presents them with no problem; others have enormous difficulty with the idea. In any case, it is best that discussion on the matter begin immediately between bride and groom and all others concerned. Don't be shy about telling both priest and minister or rabbi that you want to talk it over with them. You won't be the first couple to ask; very few of the clergy were ordained yesterday. They have dealt before with other couples who have had difficulties like your own.

If one of you is being married in a church that is not your own, you should accompany your beloved to Sunday services there a few times before your wedding. The first time you experience the church filled with people should not be your wedding day. This simple suggestion is sure to reduce anxieties when the big day comes.

Whenever it begins to seem that there are just too many rules and guidelines, try to remember that the original intent of each rule or guideline is to protect your freedom and the continued existence of the group that gave you life.

Yes, yes, you're quite correct: It can be difficult. But if you need to struggle, remember that anything that doesn't kill you is bound to make you stronger!

Parents of the Bride and Groom

The parents of the bride and groom fulfilled their major obligation long ago by bringing you into the world and assisting you on the journey toward your mutual destiny. This sounds as though it ought to be enough, but there are a few loose ends to tie up as you separate from one family and begin another. Your parents' responsibilities on this most important of occasions do not vary from what they have been doing for most of your life.

THE MOTHER OF THE BRIDE

The primary function of the bride's mother is to worry, or at least pretend to, while reassuring her daughter that there is absolutely nothing to worry about—where the wedding is concerned. Where the marriage is concerned, she is responsible for reminding the bride at least once a week (daily during the week before the wedding) that it isn't too late to back out. She is not talking about parallel parking.

The mother of the bride is allowed to blow up once a day over milk being left out or the post office being closed for Leif Ericson's birthday. For months she will have to be civil to strangers who infuriate her. Thus, the caterer gets, "Oh, no, Mr. Davenport, we understand that the icing will have to be vanilla instead of almond," which is why her beloved family members get, "Why can't people around here rinse their dishes before they put them in the dishwasher?"

THE FATHER OF THE BRIDE

While his wife should not shed tears in public until their daughter walks down the aisle (at which time it is mandatory), the father of the bride may weep while sorting through family pictures or watching Hallmark commercials.

When paying the bills, the father of the bride should be heard to sigh and comment on the low cost of aluminum extension ladders, promising to invest in one for his other daughters.

The father of the bride must be in the house or immediately available at all times on the day of the wedding. Yes, he will be in the way. Yes, his wife would probably do better without his help. But heaven help him if he should suggest that he could easily get in nine holes of golf before the wedding, even if it's true. He will never live it down. By the time the story reaches its tenth anniversary, everyone will laugh about how Bill took off to Palm Springs for a golf tournament and made it back barely in time to walk down the aisle.

THE MOTHER OF THE GROOM

It has been suggested that the job of the groom's mother is to wear beige and shut up. Usually she is more than willing to do this unless shared financial responsibility dictates shared decision making. Recognizing that discretion is the far better part of valor, the groom's mother prefers to keep her opinions to herself and save them for her own daughter's wedding.

THE FATHER OF THE GROOM

Curiously, no one can quite figure out exactly what the groom's father does. His role seems to be limited to mingling at the reception while pretending to know people he's never seen before. To this end he is advised to practice his best back slap and the following lines: "Has there been enough weather for you?" "Yes, she is lovely. We're very pleased." "I seem to have misplaced my wife."

When the parents of the bride or the groom do not find themselves married to one another on a day that beats them senseless with the sanctity of marriage, they must be happy for their children. After all it is their day, as they have so often said. As they enter yet another important stage of adulthood, they have every right to expect their elders to conduct themselves with dignity and maturity. And parents have every right to enjoy themselves and the company of their friends and relatives on this exciting day.

The Priest

Even though you minister the sacrament of matrimony to one another, the church requires the presence of one of its ordained ministers—a bishop, priest, or deacon—to witness your vows.

In approaching the priest, assume that he is still around because he wants to be helpful. Priests are usually nice guys and can be counted on to assist in planning this most important liturgy. They respond well in situations where they are called on as helpers and not as adversaries.

Ask any priest in the world when he gets his first clue that someone is too young or simply not ready for marriage. The universal answer: when mom calls to reserve the church and set up an interview. OK, OK, if you are in Tokyo and your beloved is in Kansas and you're coming home to Oregon for the wedding, we have a different case entirely. But the current thinking on the matter is that if you are old enough to get married, you are old enough to call a priest.

Actually, the first contact should not be on the phone but in person after Mass. The priest will be the guy standing by the door greeting worshippers. Just grab his hand, pump it up and down like everyone else, and introduce yourself if he does not know you. On another Sunday, reintroduce yourself and say, "I would like to call you and talk about a wedding date. When is the best time to reach you?" Don't try to make the appointment on Sunday. He has too many things going on and probably does not have his planner concealed under his vestments.

When you do reach Father Przybocki on the phone, after learning how to pronounce his name correctly, mention that you have introduced yourself on previous Sundays and which Mass you attend (you have been attending, haven't you, and not just dashing in at 10:45 to catch Father P. after the 10:00 a.m. Mass?). Then tell him that you would like to make an appointment to meet and find out what is necessary to arrange a wedding at St. Eudora's of the Burning Bush.

If you are not currently worshiping as a Catholic, you may have some difficulty securing the services of a priest. And why do you want to anyway? Catholic people have a right to the sacraments, but there seems to be no fail-safe way of proving that you are a Catholic other than celebrating the Eucharist regularly. Reciting the Apostles' Creed from memory while clutching a glow-in-the-dark rosary just doesn't cut it. If you have slipped in your practice, you can go home again, Thomas Wolfe to the contrary. Start worshiping regularly and you can be sure that all you need will be available to you.

Perhaps you have a priest friend or relative whom you would like to officiate. Most priests will be only too glad to have Father Frankie, who took the bride to the senior prom and is now ordained, come and do the honors. (If Father Frankie entered the seminary after the bride broke her engagement to him, it might be difficult for him to witness her marriage to someone else.) Remember, in all instances, to ask the pastor rather than inform. Few priests object to having others officiate in their parishes, but you won't know until you've asked.

If you are calling around to reserve a church—any church—simply because of its location, architectural splendor, or availability of off-street parking, prepare for instant rejection. Most churches—Catholic or otherwise—are quite busy ministering to the needs of their own members and have instituted policies giving those members first priority in use of the facilities.

The Best Man

The best man attends the groom and sees that all happens as smoothly as possible.

The best man begins work at the rehearsal, helping to round up the strays so that events can begin at the appointed hour.

The events preceding the wedding are often the most festive. The best man shepherds the groom throughout these festivities and makes sure that there is always a driver who has refrained from alcohol and any other debilitating substances; he sees that the one with the car keys in his pocket has 7-Up in his glass.

Should anyone decide that it would be fun to help the groom drink to excess or engage in any questionable activity that might prevent his alert attendance where and when he is expected, it is the best man's job to say no. The groom must never be put in an impossible situation. It is the best man's job to get there first and see to it that such decisions need not be made by the one about to commit himself to marriage. The best man runs interference in any situation that may hamper the groom's ability to function on the wedding day.

The best man is usually the keeper of the rings, bringing them to the ceremony and keeping them in his pocket until they are needed. He is not advised to put them both on his own fingers; they are too easily stuck there or may be lost if they fit him too loosely.

Some few best men need to hear the caution that they should take the rings out of the jeweler's box before putting them into their pockets.

It is usually the best man's task to give the priest the offering that he has been given earlier, usually by the groom. This should be done privately and discreetly. The check or cash should be in an envelope or card and never palmed off in a handclasp as one might to a bellhop who leads the happy couple to the honey-moon suite.

In most states, the signa-ture of the best man is required with that of the maid of honor and the priest on the wedding license. The best man gets the license from the bride or groom before the rehearsal, asks the priest when he would like to be given the license, and presents it at the appointed time.

It is not the best man's job to paint rude or vulgar say-ings in shaving cream on the bridal car. Those who feel so inspired should turn immediately to the essay for the ushers.

The best man is often asked to toast the bride and groom at the reception. A word of caution before you ask your cousin, fraternity brother, or army buddy to assume this responsibility. If he is at all hesitant or unsure about his ability to perform this extremely visible duty, assure him that you will find someone else who can fill in. There are times and places for long-winded stories about youthful indiscretions, punctuated with obscure inside jokes. The bachelor party comes to mind. The reception is a time for grace, eloquence, and articulate good wishes expressed to the bride and groom on behalf of friends and family members. If you're not feeling particularly creative, you can borrow this one: "To Ralph and Wanda: May they live long and prosper!" If it makes more sense to ask a favorite uncle or former lacrosse coach to do the honors, by all means do so.

If cousin Dilbert has agreed to serve as best man and really wants to be part of the festivities, but is unsure of what to write or say, buy him a book of toasts and assure him that no one will notice or care if he lifts one word for word. Suggest that he write it out so he doesn't have to rely on memory when the misty eyes of the entire family are upon him. Make sure he practices at least once before the wedding. He should hold the microphone in one hand and the script in the other. At the end of the toast, he puts the script on the table, picks up his glass, gestures toward the newly married couple, says, "To Tom and Nicole," then sits down to enjoy the rest of the day.

The Maid or Matron of Honor

Like those of the best man, the tasks of the maid or matron of honor are few but significant.

She attends the bride and sees that all happens smoothly and sensibly. Anything that might fluster the bride at this happy hour is dealt with politely and with as little fuss as possible.

The festive events preceding the wedding call for her very special attention. She ensures that there is a driver when needed who can be counted on to deliver safely those who will not be both partying and driving.

While the best man looks after the rings, the maid of honor looks after the bridal bouquet when the bride can't hold it because, for example, she is holding the groom's hand while reciting her vows. This attendant also sees that the train of the bridal gown, whenever the bride has moved to a new position, is arranged the way both the designer and God had in mind.

She joins with the best man, at least in most states, in signing the marriage license as proof positive that what you have seen exchanged—the consent and vows—is now the law.

Like the best man, the maid of honor is often asked to toast the bride and groom. Most sisters, best friends, and roomies are honored to be asked and will invest a great deal of time and angst into researching, reminiscing, writing, rewriting, and rehearsing these meaningful words of wisdom. The toast from the maid of honor often turns into a tender—and tearful—send-off for the bride. In addition to doing her best to offer succinct best wishes without blubbering incoherently (abstaining from alcohol until that point will help tremendously), the maid of honor should be prepared to offer a clean hankie to anyone at the bridal table who will need a quick mop-up after she sits down.

Bridesmaids and Groomsmen

Who needs to be there in order for you to get yourselves legally married? The two of you are the ministers of the sacrament. You're needed. The priest is necessary as the church's witness and as the state's functionary as well. Also needed are two more witnesses, usually the maid or matron of honor and the best man.

The liturgical function of these last two is small: They stand where they are told to stand, they witness the event, and, in most states, they affix their signatures to the marriage license.

As small as their function is, it is major in comparison to that of the bridesmaids and groomsmen. Outside of attending parties, wearing the appointed clothes, and having a place in the procession, these folks seem not to have a function that differs from the rest of the assembly.

There is nothing for attendants to sign other than the guest book. However, with the rest of the congregation, they join enthusiastically in prayer and song as they witness the marriage event.

On this day many brides and grooms enjoy being surrounded by their families and friends who are dressed as members of the wedding party.

There seems to be no rule about the number of those you can include as long as you realize that their function is merely decorative or supportive. Care should be taken not to exclude siblings who may be hurt when left out but who might be too shy to request that they be included. Those who cannot afford the expense should not be shy about asking to have a place as an honored guest rather than as a member of the wedding party.

Some of the attendants may be asked to give assistance to the ushers in getting the church ready and the congregation seated. In some places, the title *groomsmen* is not used: There are only bridesmaids and ushers.

There seems to be at least one story in the national press each year recounting a wedding that has just been entered in the *Guinness Book of World Records* for having included the greatest number of attendants. Perhaps one day there will be a wedding where every person in the church is in a tux or bridesmaid's dress. You, however, may wish to spend some time considering the real significance of the wedding event and the part truly played by friends and family. Invite them to be in the wedding party in numbers you consider to be in keeping with the sacramental nature of the event.

THE CREW

Musicians

The musicians who assist you in making worship should be professionals who have made music in church before. It is very difficult to take talented piano players and singers from your favorite bar and transplant them into your designated church. Their fit is not always perfect. The ministry of music is not entertainment, and folks who are completely capable in one world cannot always easily adjust to the other.

You are safest and less likely to be surprised by error or oversight if you hire the musicians who usually work in your parish or who come with the recommendation of the priest who, you will remember, attends more weddings in a season than most of us do in two-thirds of a lifetime.

Many couples ask an organist to provide their music. This need not be your only choice. Any number of instruments can serve the church at prayer. If you want a piano, harp, strings, or brass in addition to, or instead of, the organ, make the necessary arrangements with your priest and the musicians as far in advance as possible. It is likely that the parish choir director will be familiar with local musicians who are accustomed to providing liturgical music.

Ask the musicians their fee and pay them at or before the rehearsal.

The Reader

Aunt Lulu is serving punch, little cousin Jacob is watching over the guest book, second-cousin-once-removed Eunice is personal attendant to the bride, and Uncle Phil will tend bar while Aunt Elise parks cars.

We need something for brother-in-law George to do. And the only job left is reading the scriptures during the ceremony. We'll have to ask him, right?

Wrong.

For several reasons.

If George hasn't proclaimed the scriptures publicly before, asking him to solo for the first time when all the rellies are gathered is unfair. Even if he did star as Curly in the 1971 high school production of *Oklahoma!*, reading in church is a different type of affair. First, it's a ministry. Second, it requires training. Third, not all persons are disposed to or comfortable with the task.

George may not want to refuse because he wants to help and participate in the ceremony. On the other hand, if he doesn't do well, his embarrassment and your disappointment will not lessen tensions on what is usually a difficult enough day anyway.

If you don't have a family member or friend who has proclaimed scriptures for the assembly before, the wedding day is not the proper time to start. Tell the priest if you are having difficulty locating a reader and he will give you the guidance or assistance you need in recruiting the proper person.

Before you invite anyone to read at your wedding, ask the priest what particular guidelines apply at your parish. Asking in advance will make your life much easier.

The Catholic celebration of the sacrament of matrimony includes three readings from scripture—one from the Old Testament, one from the New Testament, and one from the gospel. One reader may be selected for the Old Testament reading and another to proclaim the New Testament. Or one reader may do both. In the Catholic tradition, reading the gospel before the assembly is a task reserved for the ordained.

The reader should be reconciled to the translation of the scripture provided for use in the church. He or she should not ad-lib a new translation. This too often results in mismatched verbs and nouns and a missed sense of what the scriptural author intended.

Here's an important point: There are many different translations of the scriptures, so don't ask the reader to practice from his or her own Bible. Make a copy of the readings you select from the back of this book; the translation found here is the same one found in the lectionary used in all Catholic churches. Stick with this book and avoid any confusion! It should be noted, too, that the readings should be proclaimed at the wedding from a handsome, hardcover book, not a paperback, to emphasize the solemn nature of what the assembly is about.

It should be determined whether or not book and reader will be in the entrance procession.

The reader should check the spot where he or she is to sit, with the congregation or in the sanctuary, and should try out the public address system before, during, or after the rehearsal.

The priest will give a cue when the reading is to begin at the wedding. Those who are nervous about being ready at the appropriate moment should ask what the cue will be.

Remember that to proclaim the scriptures for the Christian assembly is an honor that should not be taken lightly.

We haven't solved your problem about George. Sorry.

Ushers

Some think that ushers are groomsmen who didn't make the final cut, male friends who are honored by having some small part in the wedding ceremony.

That is not our Catholic view. We look on ushers as free labor for eight hours.

The ushers' tasks are many and varied. Much responsibility is placed on them. The ushers have more opportunity to make mistakes that will influence the flow of the ceremony than almost any other player.

The ushers' duties begin at the rehearsal, where they locate the trash cans, phones, and bathrooms that may be needed later. They listen attentively to the priest's instructions and ask for clarification when it may not be clear what is expected of them.

On the wedding day, the ushers' duties begin well before the ceremony. They are to be at the church no less than forty-five minutes before the ceremony is to begin, unless an individual parish policy differs. It is not the job of the priest to tie bow ties for ushers who haven't worn them before; when they arrive, they should already be dressed.

They make sure that the priest has help in moving any sanctuary furniture that is to be moved—and moved back as soon as the ceremony is over. Also, they see that the white aisle runner, if it is to be used, is placed securely at the head of the aisle. It is fastened down so it can be unrolled. The string for unrolling the runner is placed where it can be easily grabbed when needed and must be long enough so that a six-foot usher need not walk down the aisle stooped over in imitation of the hunchback of Notre Dame.

Some guests will insist on arriving ahead of the ushers and sitting in the back pew, aisle seat. If the ushers allow guests to sit wherever they choose, and the 170 guests are scattered across a church that seats 900, the bride will enter, think that no one has come to her wedding, be upset, and it will be the ushers' fault.

Better to plan for no disappointments. Early arrivers who sit in the back should be invited forward: "Friend, come higher! It's a large church; you'll see and hear better closer up. Will you follow me, please?"

To escort the guests to their pews, the usher extends his right elbow; the lady takes it in her left hand and proceeds. The gentleman follows and the guests are brought forward. The usher places his hand on the pew the guests are to enter, steps to one side and, after they are seated, returns to the vestibule to greet the next comers. Ushers should gently, but firmly, remind all guests to turn off cell phones and pagers. Most of us would appreciate this reminder up front, rather than face the embarrassment of our Rocky and Bullwinkle ring tone interrupting the exchange of vows.

If the usher is a woman, she does not extend her arm to those she seats, but walks by the side of the female guest, and the man follows. The procedure is then the same as outlined above.

Ushers shouldn't ask, "Friend of the bride or the groom?" but should presume that all are friends of both and should divide the guests evenly between sides unless a specific request is made.

Some guests will insist that there are bride's and groom's sides in a church. The usher's job is to humor them. Which side is which? To answer this question, God has given statues to his church. In traditional Catholic churches, there is often a statue of Mary on the left as one enters. She defines the bride's side. A statue of Joseph (or the Sacred Heart) is often on the right. He marks the gentleman's side.

After the aisle seats are filled with the early-arriving guests who want a good view, those next to arrive are seated by the side aisles.

When all the guests are seated, the grandparents are ushered in—first the paternal and then maternal grandparents of the groom, then of the bride. If parents are not in the procession, the mother of the groom is then escorted to her seat, followed by her husband. Last to enter before the games begin is the mother of the bride on the arm of the usher of her choice.

Seating arrangements for families diversified through remarriage should be planned and finalized before the rehearsal and directions given to the ushers.

The carpet is then rolled down the aisle. Don't leave the cardboard tube found in the center of the runner at the back of the church where it will be tripped over. If the ushers have attended properly to their duties, it is now only fifteen seconds before the ceremony begins and their tasks are not yet complete.

Any guests who have not yet been seated are late. They are asked politely to remain in the back (with cell phones and pagers turned off) until all in the procession have made their way into the sanctuary. The latecomers are then seated, but only by the side aisles.

The ushers may not desert the church during the ceremony to go out and smoke, send text messages, or paint vulgar sayings on the getaway car with shaving cream. This practice not only is harmful to the paint and offensive to many of those involved (is "Hot Springs Tonight!" really a destination you think needs to be broadcast to the motoring public?), but it also gets in the way of duties inside.

Should there be any difficulty during the ceremony, the priest may need to call on the ushers for help. If it is warm and windows need to be opened, for example. Or if someone faints. Or if a guest with a beeper is paged and needs to find the phone that the usher, aware of his duties, located the night before at the rehearsal. Or if the runner wrinkles and needs to be straightened. Also, some women in high heels sometimes have a difficult time walking on the plastic or paper runners and need assistance in the communion line or leaving the church.

In short, the ushers are a very significant presence and are needed far more in the church than they are in the parking lot.

Their tasks are not over when the ceremony is over. They have asked where the runner is to be stored or disposed of. They assist in moving plants or furniture as needed. Should anyone have involved himself or herself in the pagan rite of throwing rice, the ushers seek out brooms to clear away the mess so that those attending the next function in the church need not risk a fall by walking over the debris.

This having been done, the ushers brush themselves and each other off and proceed with all appropriate haste to the subsequent festivities.

Junior Members of the Party

Who is old enough to walk down the aisle ahead of you on your wedding day?

That depends. Life is not without risks, exciting and otherwise. A wedding during which everything proceeds as perfectly as planned leaves no legacy of amusing family stories that become delightfully embellished over the years.

However, professional wedding-goers can tell plenty of wedding stories that are not so amusing. These usually feature people who are inexperienced, unprepared, or not quite sure what is expected of them when the curtain goes up. Flower girls and ring bearers often find themselves in this awkward position.

More than one father of the bride has had to escort his daughter down the aisle while carrying a howling child who decided that this game wasn't much fun and she didn't want to play after all. We who are older tend to forget the terrors that children suffer.

Maybe you are ambivalent about the idea of dressing little ones like grown-ups and expecting them to conduct themselves like grown-ups. But your Aunt Lucy, who is extremely unambivalent about everything, is certain that your twin cousins would look darling as flower girl and ring bearer. If it is a risk worth taking for the sake of family peace or your own pleasure, launch little Fred and Ethel after the other attendants have made their way down the aisle, but before the maid of honor. That way, if the children balk, the maid of honor can gently take their hands and guide them to their appointed places. Aunt Lucy should sit up front next to the center aisle so the children can see her, head straight for her pew, and sit quietly by her side for the duration.

Perhaps you pale at the possibility of having to listen to six verses of what used to be your favorite hymn while your niece empties her flower basket petal by petal, returning for more when she runs out. Suggest to Aunt Lucy that you wouldn't dream of putting her and Uncle Ricky through the time and expense involved in such an endeavor. You might also suggest that Fred and Ethel dress up and assist the ushers in handing out programs, with Aunt Lucy close by. The children will not be disappointed if the importance of their job is impressed upon them.

Does this fail to answer your very simple question about who is old enough to walk down the aisle ahead of you on your wedding day? Here is a rule of thumb: Using anyone under the age of five and a half (the half in this case is significant) is risky. But perhaps you would rather rule with your heart than your thumb. Some couples take more of a chance with their thirty-year-old best man than they do with their three-year-old ring bearer.

Altar Servers

Many churches use altar servers for weddings only when the bride or groom has family members or friends they would like to honor by requesting their service for the special day.

Some priests feel they can get along well enough without servers. Others provide their own as a way for grade-schoolers either to be of service or to earn $15. Ask your priest what the custom is at your church. If you want to bring your own servers, you usually may. By now, girl servers are accepted in most places, but may be unheard of or forbidden in some parishes.

Before you make plans with cousins Angela and Angelo to come all the way from Shiremanstown to be servers in their native garb, you had better first check the local custom.

The Photographer

A visual record of your wedding is sure to be pleasing to you in years to come. A good photographer will help you preserve these memories.

As soon as you have decided on a wedding date and secured the church, select and book your photographer. If you don't get to him or her soon enough, you may be disappointed to find out that the photographer is scheduled farther in advance than you had imagined to be necessary.

Keep in mind that your wedding is a religious event and that the activities surrounding that event are to be in keeping with both the dignity of the sacrament and the place in which it is celebrated.

The church is not a studio. No altar furniture should be moved. Plan your photographs to capture your special faces and clothing and distinguishing features of the house of the church in which your wedding takes place.

Most parishes have firm rules about how much time is permitted for photography before and after the wedding. Be aware that these guidelines are for your benefit; no one wants to allow a photographer to begin taking pictures at noon for a 7 p.m. wedding. Remember that the photographer works for you and not the other way around. Remember, too, that pastors and church employees are no strangers to weddings and they know how much time is or should be taken for photographs.

Many couples have found that taking pictures before the wedding helps to relax them and allows them to get more quickly to the reception after the ceremony so that guests are not kept waiting.

Say "Pumpkin cheesecake!" as you flash those ivories.

How Much to Give Whom for Doing What

Since the celebration of your union as husband and wife inspires thoughts of love and romance and never-ending bliss, it is difficult to determine how much to pay people for their priceless services. Don't let that difficulty stop you from doing it.

Assume that it will cost to use the church even though your parents are major stockholders and faithfully spend every Saturday at church cooking, cleaning, and painting whatever needs to be cooked, cleaned, and painted. Ask the priest or someone in the parish office about the standard fee. If none is specified, don't think you are off the hook when asked to make an appropriate gift.

Before you write the check for the church, consider first: the cost of your reception, the price tag of the honeymoon, the rent for the first month in your new apartment. Ask yourself if your wedding liturgy is any less important.

The following suggestions will help you with this decision.

Do you wish to be modest? Take the cost of the groom's outfit and add it to the cost of the cake. Divide by two. This amount would be modest compensation for the time, energy, and resources used to get you up to the altar.

Want to be a bit more generous? Take the cost of the bride's clothing. Add to it the cost of the wedding photog-

raphy. Divide by two. This amount would be a more generous gift and probably a more accurate reflection of the value
of services rendered on your behalf.

If you are still unsure, consult with the priest. Though
you may find it awkward to talk about money, be assured
that he overcame his inhibitions about it long ago. A word
to the wise groom (who traditionally provides the offering):
Don't ask the priest, "How much does it cost?" because he
may well ask you, "How much is she worth?"

In some areas, the gift you make goes directly to the
parish. In some areas it is considered a gift to the priest. If
this makes a difference to you, please ask how the matter is
handled in your area. When considering what size gift to
make for services rendered and buildings used, remember
that weddings are expensive affairs.

It is the best man's task to give the priest the offering
from the bride and groom. This should be done privately
and discreetly. The check or cash should be in a card
enclosed in an envelope and never palmed off as one might
for a solicitous bellhop or maître d'.

The musicians, photographer, caterer, and other local
entrepreneurs will tell you up front what financial reim-
bursement they expect in return for helping create all this
magic. When you call upon friends to perform these tasks,
things get a little trickier but not much. If they are professionals, find out how much they customarily receive and
offer to pay it. Please remember that close friends and family members may not wish to work on your wedding day.

If your brother is arranging the flowers, your room-
mate is singing, and your uncle is witnessing your vows,
thoughtful gifts are appropriate. It is customary to buy gifts

for every member of your wedding party including the flower girl and ring bearer. Ask the priest about the standard tip for the altar servers, but if fifteen bucks apiece doesn't do it, they are too old for the job.

Prompt thank-you notes are called for all around—for both moms and dads, friends who helped in any way, and your priest who spent Friday night and most of Saturday and Sunday in church. If you are starting to turn chartreuse at the mere thought of one more thank-you note, perhaps one of you is shouldering too much of this important responsibility. Tackle them together. Isn't that the very reason you decided to wed?

THE COSTUMES

Wedding Clothes

Wedding day is dress-up day. It is a time to look and feel your very best.

The color for men who want to dress formally is black. Magenta, white, aqua, and peach tuxes and cummerbunds are formal clothes that beg to be left in the showroom. Take a long hard look at those ruffles, flourishes, and pastels. Do they detract from your handsome and happy face? Do they compete with the clean graceful lines of the bride's gown? Will the congregation assume that you are the lead guitarist for Little Archie and the Innuendos scheduled to perform at the reception?

If you are the lead guitarist for Little Archie and the Innuendos, and are required to wear a tux to work, by all means wear that tux to your wedding. It would fit well and suggest that this is how you are accustomed to dress and are not disguised for the evening as a member of European royalty. If you are not a musician or a member of European royalty, consider wedding clothes that are more a part of your life. The alternative is simple and attractive enough to be considered revolutionary.

Slacks and a blazer.

"Slacks and a blazer? Are you kidding? Where can we rent slacks and blazers?"

Don't rent. Buy.

"Buy? You mean tell all the guys in my wedding party to buy clothes for the occasion?"

Why not? Women have done it for years. Besides, a fair number of the men will already own a navy blue blazer and nice pair of grey or khaki slacks. If they don't, they should. If you're hosting an evening wedding, or your mothers insist on more formality, buy pinstripe or charcoal grey suits. A red silk tie would be a classy present from the groom. All men in the party could look well put together and handsome in clothes that can be purchased and tailored for little more than the cost of renting clothing that is usually ill-fitted and uncomfortable. Your friends will appreciate being able to make a smooth transition from your wedding to a hot date or a job interview.

"But they might not match!"

Only the Marine Corps marching band and the Rockettes need to match. Khaki is khaki and, anyway, all eyes will be on the bride.

If you decide on rented clothing, be cautious. The more your physique deviates from 5'9" and 147 pounds, the less chance you have for a perfect fit. Real clothes can be purchased and altered well in advance of the wedding wherever the purchaser happens to live. You want to see a circus? Just wait until seven men from across the country converge on the Duds for Studs Tux Emporium in your hometown three days before the wedding. You will be faced with sleeves that are too short, inseams that are too long, hems that are too obvious, and not enough time or energy to do anything about it.

If the men can be so practical, what about the women?

The bride is allowed to shell out a ridiculous sum of money for a dress that she will wear only once. Her attendants should not have to follow suit since they may very well find themselves traipsing down the aisle for multiple sisters, cousins, and softball teammates for several years to come. Every bride on the face of the planet should be forced to admit that it is nearly impossible to find one dress that truly flatters six different women. Why impose a financial hardship on your friends for the sake of a prom dress that will turn into a closet ornament the day after the wedding?

How about midlength skirts, in a seasonal fabric, with silk blouses? These would be elegant, classy, comfortable, and a sure crowd-pleaser. And the bride needn't blush when she assures her friends that they can wear these outfits again.

Another lovely and practical alternative is to ask bridesmaids to choose a seasonal formal already hanging in their closets. This approach creates a festive bouquet around the bride that will look striking and charming, both in church and at the reception, since every woman will be wearing a dress that suits her coloring and build.

Where flower girls are concerned, a truly considerate bride will not ask her four-year-old niece to spend close to twelve hours in a dry-clean-only gown that is destined to become undone, torn, or covered with lobster Newburg by the end of the day. A short, fancy party dress with ruffles, a pinafore, white tights, and patent-leather shoes will make her and everyone else more comfortable. Ribbons and bows that fit the color scheme can be added.

Plan to exercise good taste and sound judgment as you select the wardrobe for this most special day. Your wedding may be more memorable, and more imitated, than even you had thought possible.

SETTING
THE STAGE

Whose Wedding Is It Anyway?

Once you and your beloved announce your intentions, you will hear as many opinions about the wedding ceremony as you ask for and then some.

There are two prevailing philosophies about weddings.

First, there are those loving friends and relatives who peer through a lens that makes life larger than itself. Their theory is that your wedding day exists to make all your dreams come true in a lavish ceremony guaranteed to send Cinderella back to the drawing board. After all, you only get married once, the saying goes (despite statistics to the contrary), and you might as well do it right. "Right" has come to mean cramming more guests, music, flowers, liquor, food, and confusion into one day than is currently allowed by law in most states. With this philosophy, financial resources dwindle as the guest list expands.

Other friends tend to be more farsighted. They see your wedding day as the first of many in a lifetime of blessings together, and the simpler the better. Two thousand dollars for a dress she'll wear only once? Wouldn't they rather spend the money on a nice side-by-side frost-free refrigerator-freezer? You will hear about Aunt Rita who was married in the rectory wearing her WAC uniform and carrying a handful of nasturtiums from Grandma's garden, and it was a lovely ceremony, and she and Uncle Jack have been happily married for more than forty years now. (Of course when you talk to Aunt Rita, she might slip you a generous check and advise you to do it right.)

The Do-It-Right people see your wedding as a family celebration, an excellent excuse for people to get together for a great party. Expensive but well worth it.

The Hold-Your-Horses people see your wedding as a voracious beast requiring financial nourishment as each new detail is added.

Occasionally you might hear this attitude expressed by your priest. Year after year as he witnesses a seemingly endless parade of clothing, flowers, and trimmings, he wonders how struggling families can justify the expense. On the other hand, when it comes to holy orders, you'll find very few men willing to slip over to the chancery and be ordained on the floor in front of the bishop's desk.

The easiest wedding (if there is such a thing) involves multiple family members with similar ideas. It happens.

However, when you find yourselves screaming, "But it's our wedding!" it's time to examine your feelings about the wedding day.

Weddings are meant to be one-to-a-customer and as such should be custom-made with both families in mind.

Yes, you are the ones getting married. But as adults you realize that other people's plans and dreams must also be considered. It is a sad bride who after five years still pouts because she didn't get the priest she wanted. Or the flowers arrived with lavender ribbons instead of lilac. Or her best friend was too pregnant to be her matron of honor.

You have already shared many special days together and have many more to look forward to. Your wedding day will not be the first, last, or only important day in your life together as a couple.

It is only once in a lifetime, so work hard and have fun making it as lovely as possible. At the same time, take steps to ensure that your marriage will be just as special and full of joy as your wedding.

Choosing a Church

Even should you be successful in finding a priest who thinks it would be both fun for him and meaningful for you to be married while skydiving over Central Park, it is unlikely that you'll find a bishop who will permit it.

Most insist that weddings take place in a parish church or chapel, and not in a hotel ballroom or even in your parents' living room.

Before you take up the familiar battle cry, "But it's our wedding!" remember that the sacrament of matrimony is a public commitment involving more than just those immediately and intimately involved.

As a sacrament, your marriage is a visible and tangible sign to all the world of God's love. You are the light of the world, reflecting God's love for all to see. Therefore, the ceremony must be highly visible and not hidden under a bushel basket.

Your love is enshrined and your commitment is made within a Catholic liturgy. Even though it is your wedding, and all gathered pray for and with you, it is the church's liturgy. And because, in theory, all liturgy is open to the Catholic public, the church's ceremony takes place in the church's house.

These are the reasons that your priest will probably not agree to meet you on the beach, at the park, in a hot-air balloon, or anywhere other than a church or chapel that has been designated as a place for the celebration of the wedding liturgy.

Most weddings take place in the bride's church. Certainly there are other possibilities, but if you embark on a shopping expedition for a church with more parking or prettier windows, you may encounter a pastor who is less than sympathetic to your wishes.

Many parishes cannot accommodate wedding parties for those who are not members of that particular parish. This is not an obscure Catholic custom invoked by curmudgeonly pastors; it is true of most churches. If the parking lot and the windows are that important to you, join the parish (and don't be astonished when you receive envelopes and a request to serve on the parish council). Churches are built to serve the needs of the faithful community. If you have no intention of belonging to and worshiping with that community, chances are slim that you will be married there. If the parish was yours as a child and your parents are still there, tell the priest, because he may not remember you even if he knows your parents.

Some parishes require a deposit to reserve your wedding date. This deposit is refunded if everything is in working order when the wedding is over, or is applied to the fee stipulated for use of the church.

When you contract the use of the church, you will agree to the terms set by the parish office or liturgy commission. Again, these are not arbitrary rules written by a crabby priest for his own convenience. They are policies drawn up by those who regularly work in and worship in these buildings. It's wise to get the guidelines in writing before you plan to paint the pews to match the bridesmaids' gowns or install high-def, flat-screen video monitors for a PowerPoint retrospective of the lives of the bride and groom.

Some rules reinforce your own common sense regarding the behavior of the wedding party and your guests. Though you often enjoy the company of guests who eat, drink, and smoke in your house, you can understand why these activities are not permitted in a church. It is your responsibility to communicate these and other restrictions to the wedding party before the rehearsal. Other stipulations might address the use of tape on the pews, arrangement of sanctuary furniture, placement of candles and banners, which rooms are designated for use by the wedding party, how early you may arrive and how long you may stay. These guidelines are often written down on something other than stone. Ask for a printout and tuck it into your wedding file.

The rules governing the use of the church hall, if that is where you plan to hold the reception, are different in content but similar in philosophy to those governing use of the church. Your friends, who are now your guests rather than fellow worshipers, are encouraged to eat, drink, and be as merry as possible within the bounds of good taste and the boundaries of the social hall. But you can understand that the church hall should not resemble the scene of an all-night bacchanal when the preschoolers toddle in for Sunday school the next morning.

Most couples do not intentionally inconvenience the parishioners who will use the worship space when they are done with it. But it is so easy to get caught up in the excitement of the day and forget how things looked when you were still single. Written guidelines help you remember how to put things back in order.

If the pastor has a right to expect proper and safe use of the facilities, you have a right to expect some assistance in adhering to these rules. Trash receptacles should be accessible and empty. You should know where and when to obtain keys to the rooms you will need and where and when to return them. The restrooms should be clean and stocked with necessary supplies. And you should have the phone number of someone who can answer your questions patiently and completely.

Flowers, Candles, and Aisle Runners

Pick a man. Any man. Or choose a woman, but not one who has been attending weddings with an eye toward planning one of her own. Now ask this person to describe the flowers at the last wedding he or she attended.

If that last wedding played itself out in the shade of an ostentatious display of greens and cut flowers, or if the only vegetation was a single, naked carnation peeking out from the neck of a Coke bottle, chances are that your question will be answered quickly and to the accompaniment of a thigh being slapped. Most people, however, cannot answer the question.

The moral is: Flowers and plants can enhance the atmosphere when you exchange your vows. They are not central to the action; rather, they are intended to complement it. Buy, rent, or borrow accordingly.

Consider what is easily available to you seasonally. Winter brides in Minnesota have taken baskets and filled them with pine boughs. In Arizona, cactuses can be trimmed with Christmas ornaments.

Some florists will rent Boston ferns, or you can buy them and give them as gifts to particularly helpful family members when the ceremony is over. If you keep one for your own apartment, don't interpret it as a bad omen if the poor thing dies shortly after your honeymoon. Ferns seem to be more delicate than most marriages.

Looking for something borrowed, one bride used the hanging fuchsia baskets from her mother's front porch and intercepted geraniums slated to be planted in the garden. They looked quite festive in the sanctuary. Even the men noticed them.

Many churches do not permit artificial flowers of any kind. If your uncle is a silk flower broker and you had your heart set on the discount, please consult with your pastor or local liturgy committee before making any decisions. You might also ask yourself, if not your uncle, whether part of the charm of flowers is that they don't last forever.

Ask your pastor or those who assist in your church which arrangements have been the most memorable. Chances are that those most clearly remembered had a personal touch and were not lavish or outrageously expensive.

Candles and aisle runners may also be used to add a bit of pomp to your circumstances. Aisle runners were first employed in churches where floors were dirtier and colder than those of our modern churches. Though this is rarely a problem today, some families like the look of rolling out the white carpet for the bridal party.

Processing down an aisle covered with plastic is just as elegant as sitting on a couch treated the same way. On carpeted floors, a plastic runner becomes almost lethal as it is punctured by high heels. On any floor, it crinkles, wrinkles, and does not seem to know what to do with itself when the liturgy is over. Guests may kick it out of the way as they leave the church, or some helpful soul may gather it up and shove it into a corner in the vestibule before the ushers can dispose of it properly.

Linen aisle runners can be rented from your florist or a local linen-supply firm. No need to measure the length of the aisle. Your supplier should have the vital statistics on every church in town.

Candles, like children, are lovely to have around until they start leaving lasting evidence of their presence. If you want to use rented candelabra, your pastor might insist that the floor under them be protected. More plastic. The candles already in place in the sanctuary give off the same soft glow and are approved for neatness. If you provide your own candles for parish-owned fixtures, make sure that they are made to last as long as the liturgy.

Fire codes and pastoral preferences might dictate the number and placement of your candles. Know your limits before you make detailed plans.

The Procession

Getting from point B to point A is a simple matter unless point B is the back of the church, point A is the altar, and three hundred misty eyes are following your every move.

Because of the importance and festivity of the occasion, you will want to process in some fashion. The Late-for-Mass-Side-Aisle-Shuffle will not do.

Here are some of your options:

The standard lineup is for the bride to be preceded by her attendants and escorted by her father, stepfather, oldest brother, or whoever happens to be the highest ranking male in the family (figuring that out is up to you). Some might say that this is a sign that the bride is being given away. Nonsense. Catholic theology and Catholic liturgy make it clear that the man and the woman both enter marriage freely and of their own desire.

Male attendants walk with their partners or wait near the sanctuary, with the groom, for the women, and escort them to their appointed positions.

The bride and the groom may want to walk together preceded by their parents and matched pairs of attendants. This configuration neatly settles any squabbles about who will escort the bride to the sanctuary, but approach this innovation delicately. The bride and groom have the years ahead to walk side by side. For the father of the bride, this is a rare chance to get all dressed up and stand proudly next to the woman he still thinks of as his little girl. The bride who wishes to deviate slightly from tradition might approach her mother first.

Some grooms come in procession with their parents, three abreast, and wait near the sanctuary for the bride escorted by her parents. Should you decide to do it this way, it is best to avoid the linebacker lunge. Do not hook arms as a threesome and charge forward. The groom offers his arm to his mother and either holds his father's hand (practice this first—you probably have not done it since you were five years old!) or walks with dad by his side.

The bride who comes down the aisle with both parents puts one arm through her father's and holds her bouquet in that hand. She then holds her mother's hand and walks with dignity down the aisle.

If you have doubts, try out different approaches at home. This can be a lot of fun with the junior members of the family humming "Here Comes the Bride" off-key and the bride holding a medium-sized bowling trophy to simulate her bouquet. After you decide how you would like to process, check it out with the priest when you meet to plan the liturgy, then write it down, in stone, with the signatures of two sober witnesses. At the rehearsal you may not change your mind. This is for your own protection. If you seem to waver, everyone from the soloist to the best man's mother-in-law will have an opinion and you'll be there for hours rehearsing options before returning to your original idea.

An important distinction to remember is that the parade that begins your wedding is really a liturgical procession. If you want to win points with the priest, ask him whether he thinks that this procession should include the presider, the reader with the book of scriptures, and the servers bearing the cross and lighted candles. He can advise you as to the prevailing custom.

Once the liturgy is about to begin and the music starts, take a deep breath and try not to hurry. They won't start without you.

The recessional is in reverse order of the processional.

When the rites are concluded and the music begins, the groom offers his arm to his new wife; she looks radiant; they hit it.

Walk quickly, smile, and proceed to the vestibule, if that is where the receiving line will be, or to another appointed place.

The bride and groom are followed by the best man, maid of honor, other attendants, parents of the bride, parents of the groom, relatives, and other guests.

THE MUSIC

Choosing Appropriate Wedding Music

In choosing wedding music, your first responsibility is to remain faithful to the purpose and integrity of the liturgy.

This concept is not difficult to apply in other areas of our lives. Plans for a fraternity mixer are not the same as plans for a brunch honoring the new dean and her husband. The rules for soccer are different from the rules for football. We accept and delight in the differences.

Some weddings are planned as if they were theatrical productions. And, since the show is one performance only, the temptation is to pile on as much extra stuff as possible. The liturgy is likely to become buried under all the extras.

Music, unlike flowers, candles, and programs, is not merely a tuneful addition to the festivities or a pleasant form of entertainment for your guests. Music echoes our spoken prayer and is an integral part of the liturgy. It should be chosen with regard to the same standards we apply to all liturgical prayers. Catholic liturgies are carefully designed to offer glory and honor and praise and thanksgiving to God, the source and center of your lives as individuals and as a couple. Choices of sung prayer, therefore, are limited to those expressions that glorify God rather than the two of you or your parents or the Internet dating service that brought you together.

Everyone enjoys songs that evoke memories of special times in one's life. If you met and fell in love during a step-aerobics class, it is understandable that you might want to hear a retro rendition of "Uptown Girl" as the bride approaches the altar. But how will you and your fit friends resist the impulse to step, kick, turn, grapevine to the left, and cancan two three four, leaving everyone in the church completely breathless by the time the wedding party reaches the sanctuary?

And remember that what touches you will not be as touching to others. One bride had always wanted "Sunrise, Sunset" at her wedding. At the lines, "When did she get to be a beauty? When did he grow to be so tall?" the guests were amused to note that the bride (who was, in fact, quite a beauty) towered over the blushing groom, who was not very tall at all.

Many of these popular wedding tunes have been sung so often that there is no longer an ounce of sentiment left to be wrung from them. And what brings back memories to you may seem long and interminable to your grandfather who thinks that no one since Glenn Miller has written anything worth listening to.

Another responsibility you have is to a congregation of people who still think of the bride as "our little Shirley. I remember when she played the Blessed Mother in the living crèche at the cathedral." How will these people react upon hearing the soloist warble, "The first time ever I lay with you, and felt your heart so close to mine"? Your wedding is not the time to glorify the wonders of premarital sex.

This does not mean that you are limited to "In Christ There Is No East or West" and "Faith of Our Fathers." There is a wealth of music available that is both contemporary and appropriate.

For most of us, our knowledge of music is limited to whatever happens to have made the top ten for the six months before the wedding. There is much more music available that is both pleasing to you and appropriate to the occasion. Ask someone who regularly provides liturgical music in your parish if you can come to church one night after choir practice or between Masses on Sunday so that she or he can play some of your choices for you. These people are often willing to help you extend your musical horizons even if they are not playing at your wedding. Many parishes employ liturgical musicians whose tasks include helping brides and grooms select the music for their weddings. Do not be shy in seeking to set up an appointment.

Perhaps there is a music store nearby that will have discs available with some of the choices. Some parish musicians also have resources so you can hear what they are able to do. Ask. Don't forget to search the Internet, which often provides a rich bounty.

To ease your way into choosing liturgical music, start with scripture. Select first the psalm you will use between the first (Old Testament) and second (New Testament) readings. Recall King David dancing before the ark of the covenant and keep in mind that his psalms were written as poems and songs. Perhaps you have a favorite psalm that would be appropriate for the occasion. One bride and groom, still rejoicing in the Easter feast that preceded their wedding, used the Easter psalm, "This is the day the Lord has made; let us rejoice and be glad in it," with a musical setting familiar in their parish. There may be hymns that you have enjoyed for years without realizing that they were psalms.

The psalm having been selected, advance directly to the remaining parts of the liturgy you might want to emphasize with music. See "Planning a Wedding Liturgy" on page 89 for guidelines concerning music for each part of the ceremony, and consult your local liturgical musicians for suggested selections.

There are any number of instrumentals that are suitable for use. If you are unfamiliar with classical music, you might call your church organist and ask to visit between services on Sunday or before or after choir rehearsal to determine whether he or she would be willing to play samples of what you might select for use on your wedding day.

What about songs that have always been your favorite but haven't yet found a home in the scheme of things? Consider using them: to begin the rehearsal, at the rehearsal dinner or reception, in church before the ceremony as the guests are being seated, or after the ceremony while guests are waiting to go through the receiving line.

Does all this help you to understand why your pastor placed his head on his desk and wept when you asked to have the theme from *Titanic* played after the exchange of vows?

THE SCRIPT

Tradition

Dear Miss Manners,
> **Who says there is a "right" way of doing things and a "wrong" way?**

Gentle Reader,
> **Miss Manners does. You want to make something of it?**
> (*Miss Manners' Guide to Excruciatingly Correct Behavior*)

It's your wedding and you should do what you want to do. And I'm sure that what you want to do is offend as few people as possible.
> (*The Almost Always Right Rev. William C. Graham*)

You have chosen a ceremony laden with Catholic prayer, ritual, and symbolism. If this were not your preference, you would have contacted a judge, a justice of the peace, or a ship's captain.

This wedding of yours has both a very private significance and a very public face. How do you approach the task of planning a liturgy that meets the requirements of the church, the requests of relatives, and your own desires?

First a word from one of our major sponsors—tradition. Tradition, a benevolent despot, insists things be done her way just because things have always been done her way. However, tradition did not come to power spontaneously or of her own accord. Tradition governs ceremonies and rituals generated by the human need to celebrate and commemorate as members of a community. Surely we can (and do) name our children, express sorrow for sins, enter adulthood, declare love for our partner, and mourn our dead in private. But there is a common desire to share these events with others. It would be difficult if not impossible to do these things publicly without tradition to guide and shape our rituals.

For instance, can you imagine what christenings would be like if there were no ritual to follow? Maybe you would choose a convenient Sunday, bring Homer Jr. to Mass, stand up after the sign of peace, and get the attention of the priest and congregation. "We just wanted everyone to know that we have a new baby, and his name is Homer Jr., and we'd like him to be accepted as a member of this Christian community. Is that OK with everyone? Good. Thanks."

Planning a liturgy within established guidelines is tough enough. It would be a lot harder if the priest told your parents, "I'll be there at six o'clock. You guys just let me know where you want me to stand and what you want me to say."

The customs contained in all our rituals were included for reasons that were perfectly logical at an earlier time. Now some are delightful remnants of old superstitions, while others have real historic or liturgical significance and are not done away with lightly.

Perhaps you want it all. You've always wanted it all—the white dress, the rings, the rice, "Oh Promise Me," the whole works. Fine.

On the other hand, perhaps you or your friends or family members insist that customs that do not reflect modern reality have no place in a modern ceremony.

Maybe there are objections to the idea of a bride who is wrapped like an expensive gift and presented to a waiting groom. Some will challenge suggested scripture readings or scorn such practices as pelting one another with rice, garters, and bouquets. (And far too few of us object to the curious custom of getting completely trashed at the bachelor party.)

Now a word from our second major sponsor—compromise. Compromise gets a good workout in planning a wedding, preparing both of you for what lies ahead for the rest of your lives.

Where your wedding is concerned, you must consider: your own desires, because this is one of the most important days in your life; love for your parents, because this is an important day in their lives; and a sense of history, because you are a special couple in a long line of special couples to pledge your love in this ceremony. The liturgy becomes more meaningful when you include external expressions that show you are celebrating in the same way your ancestors did and your descendants will.

As you challenge these external expressions, ask yourselves what they really mean and whether you will be able to eliminate them gracefully.

For instance, why would anyone think that the father of the bride is giving his daughter away? The church asks both groom and bride long before the wedding to sign a statement that you enter into marriage of your own free will. Few brides object to being escorted down the aisle on the arm of a handsome man. Before you insist that the man be the groom, how do you plan to break the news to the father who has dreamed for twenty-seven years of walking down the aisle with his only daughter? Good luck.

As far as scripture is concerned, many (including feminists) see the need to proclaim the scriptures exactly as written to remind us of our heritage and to demonstrate the inadequacy of human language in describing God's love.

Sometimes liturgical prayers seem inadequate, too. Perhaps they do not seem to express your understanding of the nature of God or your relationship with him. Keep in mind that the church is charged with the overwhelming task of developing prayers that speak of the faith, hope, and love of more than one billion Catholics worldwide. As the church strives to be one, holy, catholic, and apostolic, her prayers used for worship must reflect unity and a common sense of purpose and belief.

Private expressions of prayer change and develop as personal faith deepens and matures. Changes in liturgical prayer take place much more slowly and deliberately because so many people are affected by the change. This is why we make room in our lives for both private and congregational prayer.

All human utterances are flawed by their very nature. We turn constantly to the Holy Spirit to guide us and give us patience as we struggle to pray with one voice.

If it seems necessary to do away with old customs and institute new ones, remember to choose your battles wisely. And remember that your values and convictions are more accurately and lastingly reflected in your marriage than in your wedding liturgy.

The Lofty Side of Marriage

Catholics have a solemn view of marriage. This is reflected in the church's use of phrases like *irrevocable bond, permanent commitment, total fidelity, unbreakable oneness,* and *holy mystery* when speaking of the marriage relationship. Some may be confused about what all this really means. The church's prayer, however, reveals what the church teaches. These prayers show not the church laws governing marriage, but the church's high regard for the vocation of marriage.

If you and your beloved, or other interested parties, are looking for a short and sweet pronouncement on the Catholic theology of marriage, you need only to spend a few minutes studying the nuptial blessing. All liturgical prayers and blessings are statements about the beliefs and hopes of individuals as well as the universal church.

What you see printed for the church to pray is what the church believes.

"Let us pray to the Lord for Melissa and Dylan..."

The priest begins with words so familiar that sometimes the formula fails to register, but this introduction is a significant part of the blessing. An invitation to the congregation is a reminder that marriage is not just a private event. Until this point, you might think that your feelings for each other have been a romantic secret. Now your relationship takes on a public significance that goes beyond wearing wedding rings and signing "Mr. and Mrs." in the hotel guest book. The special gift that married people enjoy becomes a sign of God's love to his people.

"…who come to God's altar at the beginning of their married life so that they may always be united in love for each other."

Not only is your declaration of love and commitment made before Mom, Dad, Nana, Granddad, Cousin Alyce, and countless other members of the Keating and Gagne families, it is made before God. Your vows have both a public face and private significance. Makes you stop and think about it a little bit, doesn't it!

"Father, to reveal the plan of your love…"

God, who does not use the awesome power of his love lightly or without purpose, provides within marriage a means of sharing his love. As you wonder whether you really need a wedding ceremony and a marriage license to demonstrate your love commitment, it might seem as though marriage was instituted by a shrewd entrepreneur who decided to package some of this love floating around and market it to florists, dressmakers, caterers, and ring engravers. The Christian belief is that marriage is a gift from God, who is the source of all love. As Christians, you have made the joint decision not only to accept this gift, but also to cherish and nurture it all the days of your lives.

"…you made the union of husband and wife an image of the covenant between you and your people."

When God makes promises to his people, he doesn't fool around. A covenant is not merely a contract with an option to renew after three years. God, who remains faithful no matter how often his people fail him, asks you to remain faithful to each other in good times and in bad. Because married love is a sign of God's undying love, you promise permanence as well as love to one another.

"In the fulfillment of this sacrament, the marriage of a Christian man and woman is a sign of the marriage of Christ and the Church."

All sacraments are outward expressions of God's love. Marriage remains a sacrament not just on your wedding day but on every day of your married life. As Christ ministers to his people through the church, you constantly minister to one another and become witnesses of God's love through the sacrament of matrimony.

It is especially appropriate to note that you are the ministers of the sacrament on the wedding day, with the priest as a witness. After the wedding, you will minister the sacrament daily in your new vocation as husband and wife.

And what a fun and challenging ministry it can be. The fulfillment of the sacrament begins with the exchange of vows and continues as you argue over wallpaper patterns, make love while the kids are watching cartoons, plan your dream vacation, volunteer at the food shelf together, comfort and encourage each other in times of sadness, celebrate in times of joy, and forgive each other again and again, building and strengthening your friendship day after day.

"Lord, grant that as they begin to live this sacrament they may share with each other the gifts of your love and become one in heart and mind as witnesses to your presence in their marriage."

You will not always feel the presence of God in your marriage. At times you will feel as though the First Federal Savings and Loan has more of a presence in your marriage than God does. Occasionally, God will seem temporarily out of town as you struggle to live with a teething two-year-old, a half-remodeled kitchen, or an elderly relative.

As Christian people, you come to the altar of God to ask his blessing on your marriage. You are reminded by the church to turn constantly toward God so that his love may be reflected in your sacrament.

"Help them create a home together and give them children to be formed by the gospel and to have a place in your family."

Many people hear this line and pounce. "Aha! That's all the church really cares about! Babies! Those celibate men in Rome can't wait till she starts turning out potential parishioners."

The church recognizes that marriage has its own dignity for the partners while they are husband and wife as well as when they become mom and dad. The careful wording of this part of the blessing indicates that, though the other purposes of marriage are not to be considered less important, children are also gifts from God to parents who become co-creators with him.

God relies on the cooperative love of a man and a woman to enlarge his family. And he trusts that your vow of permanent love will ensure a stable, loving environment for your family, when it includes just the two of you and when it grows to include children.

"Give your blessings to Melissa, your daughter, so that she may be a good wife and mother, caring for the home, faithful in love for her husband, generous and kind."

The nuptial blessing used to be called the bride's blessing and it ended here. Through this, the church seemed to teach that the bride had a long hard road ahead of her and she was going to need all the help she could get.

This part of the blessing recalls the bride's baptism, and her own considerable dignity as a daughter of God. It also lists prominent examples of the virtues of the holy women whose praises are sung in the scriptures.

"Give your blessing to Dylan, your son, so that he may be a faithful husband and a good father."

Does the groom get cheated here? After petitioning for blessings on the bride, is the church asking God a bit less for the guy standing next to her? Maybe the people writing the prayer figured it's hard enough just being a faithful husband and good father. And in twenty-first century America, they may be right. But it also seems to be taken for granted that a faithful husband will also be generous and kind and care for the home.

"Father, grant that as they come together to your table on earth, so they may one day have the joy of sharing your feast in heaven."

Sacraments give the grace and strength needed for the journey until God's people are united with him in heaven. This is one of the strongest statements of faith you can make as individuals and as a couple. The delight you find in one another is but a brief taste and promise of what waits for you at the banquet in the new and heavenly Jerusalem.

These blessings are not bestowed on you by the church; rather, the church joins with your friends and family in asking God to grant these many blessings. And, as do all faithful Christians, **"we ask this through Christ our Lord. Amen."**

Planning a Wedding Liturgy

Every week, Catholics all over America "go to church." Most of us don't talk about celebrating the Eucharist, joining the assembly to greet the Lord present in word and sacrament, or participating in the saving mysteries as God's priestly people.

So when wedding time rolls around and we are invited to "plan a liturgy," pulses might quicken and stomachs tighten in anticipation of an activity that is usually reserved for experienced professionals.

Priests, deacons, and liturgical musicians spend years in preparation for the job of planning and leading worship services. There is no reason that you should feel entirely and immediately comfortable in taking on the role of liturgy planner of the hour.

The amount of planning you do will depend largely on your willingness to enter into the process coupled with parish custom and the willingness of your priest to be open to your participation.

Bride and groom come together in a church to speak their vows. Bride and groom should share in the opportunity to plan the liturgy that surrounds those vows.

Remember as you begin the process that bride and groom confer the sacrament upon one another as they pledge their love before the altar of God. You plan this liturgical moment insofar as you are able to select scripture, prayers, blessings, and music that will help both you and the assembly clearly understand and celebrate the sacrament of matrimony.

As you rejoice in your love and invite the assembly to rejoice with you, remember also that you come together in praise of God and in thanksgiving for the gift of the love you have found and fashioned. It is always God who is worshiped and praised, not the bridal couple.

Perhaps the best place to begin is with scripture. Together read the scripture passages appointed for use during the wedding liturgy. Together read the comments provided. Discuss your favorites and give reasons for your choices. Point out to one another those ideas you consider objectionable to you. If you are uneasy discussing scripture with one another, discuss that too.

You do justice to the richness of the word of God to consider your choices well in advance of the wedding day. Read them often until they are familiar to both of you and clear choices can be made. Then, during the liturgy, the proclamation of scripture becomes also a proclamation of what you believe, and of your hopes for married life.

Planning ahead also prevents the following conversation from taking place in the car on the way to the rehearsal:

"Good grief, we don't have the readings picked out yet!"

"I thought you were going to do that!"

"No, remember, I said I would design the program if you would look at the readings and let me know what sounded good."

"Well, we have to have *something*. Where's that book?"

"I gave it to you to show your mom the chapter on flower girls. Where did you put it?"

"I never took it out of the car. It must be here somewhere."

"Here it is. Now let's see...scripture, scripture. Here we go."

"Hurry and pick something. We're almost there. Just don't pick the one about wives and submission. All of Grandma's book-club friends will be there."

If you take time to study the selections and choose the readings together, you will find yourselves forever exchanging smiles when you hear the passages of scripture that now hold special meaning for you as a couple.

Next, consider other parts of the liturgy, both spoken and sung. They are:

PROCESSIONAL

This selection should be an instrumental. Having a song sung while you come down the aisle calls for too many senses to be pressed into service at one time by the assembly. Liturgical processions can be lots of fun and most people want to watch and point to familiar faces. Allow your musicians to play as you enter and save the singing for another moment. For the order of the processional, see page 67.

HYMN

An opening hymn after the bridal procession has moved into the sanctuary is a good idea for several reasons. It sets the proper tone immediately, letting the guests know that this is a sacramental encounter that they have been invited to witness. Thus they are to join in prayer for the success of this union of the bride and groom. Inviting them to sing is inviting them to pray twice.

This is a particularly good opportunity for those wedding parties in which all are not Catholic. If you choose a hymn that you know to be a favorite of those family members from another church, you are sure to impress them with your thoughtfulness and hospitality.

OPENING PRAYER

As you read the options given, try to discern what the church suggests in the statements made in these prayers. One of the ancient maxims of the Church is *lex orandi, lex credendi,* "the law of prayer establishes the law of belief"— which is to say that if you want to discover what the church teaches about something in particular, look carefully at the prayers assigned for use on those occasions. The church's theology finds its very clear expression in the wedding prayers.

OLD TESTAMENT READING

Choose and deliver this to the reader well before the rehearsal. See scripture selection on pages 122–36.

PSALM

Choose a psalm set to music (see pages 156–65) that can be sung by the congregation or the soloist. The refrains to many psalms are simple tunes that can easily be sung by a congregation led by a cantor who solos the verses.

NEW TESTAMENT READING

Also choose and deliver this to the reader in advance of the rehearsal. Your celebrant will also want to know which readings you have selected. See pages 136–55.

ALLELUIA

With this acclamation, used in every season except Lent (when another acclamation is substituted), the assembly greets the gospel in song, repeating the refrain after the cantor. See page 166.

GOSPEL

In the Catholic tradition, the gospel is proclaimed only by an ordained person, but, as with the other scripture readings, you are free to choose one that reflects your understanding of the sacrament. See pages 167–80.

HOMILY

The preacher will want to prepare a homily that is a reflection on the message contained in the word of God. This is a good reason to inform him promptly of your decisions about scripture.

EXCHANGE OF VOWS

When your grandparents were married, the prevailing custom was for the bride and groom to get dressed to the nines and gather their friends and family in a public place of worship. Then, when it came to the very reason for all the hoopla, they turned their backs on everyone, went into a huddle with the priest, mumbled a few words, and that was it. They were hitched. The backs of bridal gowns are so lovely because traditionally that was all anyone ever saw during the wedding.

Today's brides and grooms are encouraged to show their nervous but smiling faces for all to see as they exchange vows and rings.

After all, this is where it all comes together. This is where months of preparation and planning meet a lifetime of better and worse, sickness and health, good times and bad. You want people to pay attention to this sacred moment, and they want to see and hear what's going on.

Therefore, more and more priests are suggesting that when you exchange vows, you turn slightly toward one another while facing the congregation. The priest stands between the two front pews and witnesses your exchange along with the rest of the congregation, who will appreciate a clear view of the main event.

Next, you will decide how to recite your vows. It's another one of those details that seems so simple when you watch someone else do it (after all, how hard can it be to memorize forty words?), and you want it to look that way when you do it too.

If you choose to memorize and recite them one to

another, the priest will be there with his book open to the right page in the event that your memory stumbles.

You might also choose to read the vows directly from the book.

Or you can let the priest ask the traditional questions to which you reply, "I do."

Which option is preferable depends largely on your personalities. If you can memorize or read well, it would certainly be appropriate to proclaim the vows to each other since you confer the sacrament on one another. In this way, your effort adds emphasis to the holy words you speak.

If the very thought of reading or speaking in public causes endless distress, play it safe and choose to respond, "I do," in response to the priest's questions.

Repeating the vows line by line after the priest is usually not a good choice. It seems to suggest that neither of you can read.

In all cases, remain sensitive to the feelings of your partner. If what you would like to do is something that she or he is unable or unwilling to do, this is one more opportunity for you to compromise, or give in, cheerfully. ("I'll memorize the vows if you write all the thank-you notes and polish the silver twice a year" is not a compromise!)

Few couples ask to write their own vows, because what they end up with is a longer, more complicated version of the simple and noble promises prescribed by the church. Some priests will allow you to add a sentence or two. Most are convinced that the vows as they are written are almost impossible to improve upon.

The three choices of vows for Catholics in the United States are printed on pages 105–6. Study them carefully and talk with your priest about which vows you have chosen and how you would like to exchange them.

BLESSING AND EXCHANGING OF RINGS

The symbolic significance of your wedding rings finds its expression in the prayer of blessing over them. If you ever wonder what the church teaches about anything in particular, look for the prayers provided to be said at the time or over the objects in question.

Over the rings the priest might say, "May the Lord bless these rings which you give to each other as signs of your love and fidelity."

The rings should get into the church in the best man's right front pocket. Tell him to take the rings out of the box first.

The maid of honor should probably not carry the rings. She usually doesn't have pockets and is busy enough carrying her own flowers and fixing the bridal train. The maid of honor also takes care of the bride's flowers as the vows are recited.

Some want a ring bearer. Fine. Tell your mother not to use her best Girl Scout knot tying the rings onto the pillow. More than one keepsake has been destroyed that way and more than two rings have been sent accidentally flying across the church when released from a tightly tied knot. A bow will hold them nicely.

Before the ceremony, the bride puts her engagement ring on her right hand. This leaves her left ring finger free to receive her wedding band from her beloved, after which she will lovingly give him his ring in the same way. Later, the engagement ring is moved to its permanent home outside the wedding band. The idea is that a vein runs directly from that finger to the heart, and if it keeps you thinking of your beloved and the sanctity of your vows, who is to dismiss the idea?

Your fingers may not fit the rings as well on the wedding day as they did when you first tried them on. The ring may require a bit of tugging to get it where it belongs. When you slip it onto your beloved's finger, push it only as far as the second knuckle if the fit is snug. Then that sweaty hand can retreat to its owner who will discreetly push the ring the rest of the way. No need for the congregation to see your first struggle when you have been married all of ninety seconds.

Before selecting music for this important moment in the liturgy, reread the actual vows and the formula for the blessing and exchange of rings. Take note of the noble simplicity of this rite. You do not want to overshadow your promises with lyrics that are trite or not in keeping with the theology of the vows.

THE KISS

After the exchange of vows and rings, you may wish to exchange a kiss. Ask the priest if this is customary in your area.

If so, the bride might not want the priest to say to the groom, "You may now kiss the bride." After all, the groom has probably not asked for priestly permission up until this point. And, if he can offer her kiss to her new husband, to whom else may he offer a kiss of hers? "You may now kiss the groom"? Not much better.

"You may now exchange a kiss" is a good statement that indicates that the kiss puts a seal on what has already been spoken. The kiss also calls to mind that marriages must be both *ratum et consummatum,* which is to say both ratified (which you do through your vows) and consummated (which generally needs little prompting from the church).

The kiss is not to be a lengthy demonstration of what is to follow as soon as the guests go home. Some priests have been heard to suggest, "You may now exchange a chaste kiss."

PRESENTATION AND PREPARATION OF THE GIFTS

If the Eucharist is celebrated, the gifts of bread and wine may be presented to the priest by friends or family members. This activity may be accompanied by a hymn. Instrumental music is suggested if a vocal solo was used after the vows.

PREFACE

If the Eucharist will be celebrated within the wedding liturgy, you will need to select, or have selected for you, a preface that begins the eucharistic prayer. From the options found on pages 111–13, determine which most clearly expresses what you understand yourselves to be about as you begin married life.

Many people consider it awkward to ask Catholics to kneel and all others to sit during the eucharistic prayer. And it would seem not quite polite to tell those who are not Catholic, "Well, when in Rome...." Some suggest that all of these considerations are best met by inviting the entire congregation to stand throughout the eucharistic prayer.

An ancient custom might be invoked that forbids kneeling on days of great joy; and, you might point out, standing is the posture of the resurrection people. Discuss this with the priest.

ACCLAMATIONS DURING THE EUCHARISTIC PRAYER

Musical settings for the acclamations during the eucharistic prayer should also be selected with care. These are the Holy, Holy, the Memorial Acclamation, and the Amen. Your best bet here might be to seek out your parish musician and find out which settings are most commonly sung in your parish. Stick with these. At least the guests from your home church will know these important parts of the common prayer. If the soloist is not familiar with the acclamations, insist that she or he learn them so that the congregation can have a leader.

LORD'S PRAYER

The Lord's Prayer is the only prayer that Jesus gave us. Christians are called to make this prayer three times daily, and whenever the church gathers, it is said in unison. It can never be taken from the assembly. Therefore, it is inappropriate to have it sung as a solo during your wedding. Also, it might be the only prayer that the entire congregation will offer together since it is known by Christians of every denomination.

If you wish the entire congregation to sing the Lord's Prayer, select a setting that is familiar to most people in your area.

If it was soloed at your mom's wedding and she insists on having it at yours, you might suggest that it be sung either before the ceremony or during communion in addition to being sung or recited at the appointed time.

NUPTIAL BLESSING

Choose the blessing from the options listed on pages 113–17 that most clearly expresses your hopes for the union you begin as husband and wife before the altar of God.

SIGN OF PEACE

Jesus promised us peace. Hopeful always, the assembly exchanges with one another some sign of this promise. It is important that you not confuse this ritual with the receiving line. Ask your priest what the custom is in your parish, but note that you should not seek to greet every family member or guest in the church with the sign of peace. And do make your pilgrimage together as you embrace both moms and dads, for example. You are a couple now.

COMMUNION

Will you need to appoint eucharistic ministers to assist with the distribution of communion? Will all communicants be offered communion from the cup? Ask what your parish customs are and what considerations you need to make. Decide also whether to have a hymn, solo, or instrumental selection.

BLESSING AND DISMISSAL OF THE CONGREGATION

Their happy task of witnessing your vows is now complete. The assembly is sent in peace to continue the celebration.

RECESSIONAL

Exit the church in the reverse order of the processional, led by the newly married couple and accompanied by instrumental music.

To Eucharist or Not to Eucharist?

Whether or not to celebrate the Eucharist at your wedding may be a question that consumes many hours for some couples and their parents.

Are the bride and groom both Catholics who worship regularly? There seems to be every reason then to ask that your vows be exchanged at Mass unless you live in an area where the shortage of priests makes this impossible.

If either the bride or the groom is not a Catholic, it can be presumed that about half of the guests will also not be Catholic. You might then observe that the Eucharist is a sign of unity. But when only half of the bridal couple and half of the congregation will approach the eucharistic table, our differences rather than our unity may find themselves highlighted. Perhaps it would be better to exchange your vows in a ceremony outside of Mass. Those Catholics who don't want to consider the sacrament of marriage outside the context of the Eucharist can perhaps be invited to a private Mass in the parish church earlier on the wedding day or the day before.

The feelings of the non-Catholic party must always be respected in this discussion even before the opinion of your grandmother.

If you choose to celebrate the Eucharist on this special day, what about those who are not Catholic come communion time? This is not a question about separating sheep from goats, but is a question of eucharistic hospitality that Christian denominations answer differently.

Catholics teach that because the Eucharist is a sign of our unity and the Christian church is splintered today rather than united, we do not celebrate the Eucharist together.

Many Protestant denominations, on the other hand, say that precisely because the Eucharist is a sign of unity, all baptized persons are invited to celebrate it together as a sign of our hope until the day we are united as one flock with one shepherd.

One can hardly argue with either of these stands; it looks like a case of two different answers to a question with both answers correct. The best course is to listen to the teachings of our own church and to respect the practices of the other churches into which we are invited.

Some people will tell you that all who participate in a Catholic wedding are expected to receive communion. This is obviously untrue and contrary to Catholic practice. How would you like to be a Jew or a Muslim or a Buddhist invited to a Catholic wedding and have that twist thrown at you?

It is best to discuss these issues with your priest. He can help you better to understand Catholic practice and where and how it differs from practices of the other churches in your area. He can also help you to interpret particular guidelines in your church that may differ in their emphases from diocese to diocese.

The Rite of Marriage

All stand, including the bride and bridegroom, and the priest addresses them in these or similar words:

My dear friends, you have come together in this church so that the Lord may seal and strengthen your love in the presence of the Church's minister and this community. Christ abundantly blesses this love. He has already consecrated you in baptism and now he enriches and strengthens you by a special sacrament so that you may assume the duties of marriage in mutual and lasting fidelity. And so, in the presence of the Church, I ask you to state your intentions.

The priest then questions them about their freedom of choice, faithfulness to each other, and the acceptance and upbringing of children.

N. and N., have you come here freely and without reservation to give yourselves to each other in marriage?

Will you love and honor each other as man and wife for the rest of your lives?

The following question may be omitted if, for example, the couple is advanced in years.

Will you accept children lovingly from God, and bring them up according to the law of Christ and his Church?
Each answers the question separately.

CONSENT

The priest invites them to declare their consent.

Since it is your intention to enter into marriage, join your right hands, and declare your consent before God and his church.

They join hands.

The bridegroom says:

I, N., take you, N., to be my wife. I promise to be true to you in good times and in bad, in sickness and in health. I will love you and honor you all the days of my life.

The bride says:

I, N., take you N., to be my husband. I promise to be true to you in good times and in bad, in sickness and in health. I will love you and honor you all the days of my life.

If, however, it seems preferable for pastoral reasons, the priest may obtain consent from the couple through questions. First he asks the bridegroom:

N., do you take N. to be your wife? Do you promise to be true to her in good times and in bad, in sickness and in health, to love her and honor her all the days of your life?

The bridegroom: **I do.**

Then he asks the bride:

N., do you take N. to be your husband? Do you promise to be true to him in good times and in bad,

in sickness and in health, to love him and honor him all the days of your life?

The bride: **I do.**

In the dioceses of the United States, the following form may also be used:

> **I, N., take you, N., for my lawful wife, to have and to hold, from this day forward, for better, for worse, for richer, for poorer, in sickness and in health, until death do us part.**

> **I, N., take you N., for my lawful husband, to have and to hold, from this day forward, for better, for worse, for richer, for poorer, in sickness and in health, until death do us part.**

If it seems preferable for pastoral reasons for the priest to obtain consent from the couple through questions, in the dioceses of the United States the following alternative form may be used:

> **N., do you take N. for your lawful wife (husband), to have and to hold, from this day forward, for better, for worse, for richer, for poorer, in sickness and in health, until death do you part?**

The bride (bridegroom): **I do.**

Receiving their consent, the priest says:

> **You have declared your consent before the Church. May the Lord in his goodness strengthen your consent and fill you both with his blessings.**

What God has joined, men must not divide.

R. Amen.

BLESSING AND EXCHANGE OF RINGS

Priest:

> May the Lord bless ✠ these rings which you give to each other as the sign of your love and fidelity.

R. Amen.

Or:

> Lord, bless these rings which we bless ✠ in your name.
>
> Grant that those who wear them may always have a deep faith in each other.
>
> May they do your will and always live together in peace, good will, and love.
>
> We ask this through Christ our Lord.

R. Amen.

Or:

> Lord, bless ✠ and consecrate N. and N. in their love for each other.
>
> May these rings be a symbol of true faith in each other, and always remind them of their love.
>
> We ask this through Christ our Lord.

R. Amen.

The bridegroom places his wife's ring on her ring finger.

He may say:

> N., take this ring as a sign of my love and fidelity. In the name of the Father, and of the Son, and the Holy Spirit.

The bride places her husband's ring on his ring finger.

She may say:

> N., take this ring as a sign of my love and fidelity. In the name of the Father, and of the Son, and of the Holy Spirit.

OPENING PRAYERS

> Father,
> you have made the bond of marriage
> a holy mystery,
> a symbol of Christ's love for his Church.
> Hear our prayers for N. and N.
> With faith in you and in each other
> they pledge their love today.
> May their lives always bear witness
> to the reality of that love.
> We ask this through our Lord Jesus Christ,
> your Son,
> who lives and reigns with you and the Holy Spirit,
> one God, for ever and ever.

Or:

> Father,
> hear our prayers for N. and N.,

who today are united in marriage before
your altar.
Give them your blessing,
and strengthen their love for each other.
We ask this through our Lord Jesus Christ, your
Son,
who lives and reigns with you and the Holy Spirit,
one God, for ever and ever.

Or:

Almighty God,
hear our prayers for N. and N.,
who have come here today
to be united in the sacrament of marriage.
Increase their faith in you and in each other,
and through them bless your Church (with
Christian children).
We ask this through our Lord Jesus Christ, your
Son,
who lives and reigns with you and the Holy Spirit,
one God, forever and ever.

Or:

Father,
when you created mankind
you willed that man and wife should be one.
Bind N. and N. in the loving union of marriage;
and make their love fruitful
so that they may be living witnesses
to your divine love in the world.
We ask this through our Lord Jesus Christ, your
Son,

who lives and reigns with you and the Holy Spirit,
one God, for ever and ever.

PRAYERS OVER THE GIFTS

Lord,
accept our offering
for this newly-married couple, N. and N.
By your love and providence you have brought
   them together;
now bless them all the days of their married life.
We ask this through Christ our Lord.

Or:

Lord,
accept the gifts we offer you
on this happy day.
In your fatherly love
watch over and protect N. and N.,
whom you have united in marriage.
We ask this through Christ our Lord.

Or:

Lord,
hear our prayers
and accept the gifts we offer for N. and N.
Today you have made them one in the sacrament
   of marriage.
May the mystery of Christ's unselfish love,
which we celebrate in this Eucharist,
increase their love for you and for each other.
We ask this through Christ our Lord.

PREFACES

Father, all-powerful and ever-living God,
we do well always and everywhere to give you
   thanks.
By this sacrament your grace unites man and
   woman
in an unbreakable bond of love and peace.
You have designed the chaste love of husband
   and wife
for the increase both of the human family
and of your own family born in baptism.
You are the loving Father of the world of nature;
you are the loving Father of the new creation of
   grace.
In Christian marriage you bring together the two
   orders of creation:
nature's gift of children enriches the world
and your grace enriches also your Church.
Through Christ the choirs of angels
and all the saints
praise and worship your glory.
May our voices blend with theirs
as we join in their unending hymn:

Or:

Father, all-powerful and ever-living God,
we do well always and everywhere to give you
   thanks
through Jesus Christ our Lord.
Through him you entered into a new covenant
   with your people.

You restored man to grace in the saving mystery
   of redemption.
You gave him a share in the divine life
through his union with Christ.
You made him an heir of Christ's eternal glory.
This outpouring of love in the new covenant
   of grace
is symbolized in the marriage covenant
that seals the love of husband and wife
and reflects your divine plan of love.
And so, with the angels and all the saints in
   heaven
we proclaim your glory
and join in their unending hymn of praise:

Or:

Father, all-powerful and ever-living God,
we do well always and everywhere to give you
   thanks.
You created man in love to share your divine life.
We see his high destiny in the love of husband
   and wife,
which bears the imprint of your own divine love.
Love is man's origin,
love is his constant calling,
love is his fulfillment in heaven.
The love of man and woman
is made holy in the sacrament of marriage,
and becomes the mirror of our everlasting love.
Through Christ the choirs of angels
and all the saints

praise and worship your glory.
May our voices blend with theirs
as we join in their unending hymn:

NUPTIAL BLESSINGS

I.

My dear friends, let us turn to the Lord and pray that he
will bless with his grace this woman (or N.) now married in Christ to this man (or N.) and that (through the
sacrament of the body and blood of Christ,) he will
unite in love the couple he has joined in this holy bond.

All pray silently for a short while. Then the priest extends
his hands and continues:

> Father, by your power you have made everything
>   out of nothing.
> In the beginning you created the universe
> and made mankind in your own likeness.
> You gave man the constant help of woman
> so that man and woman should no longer be two,
>   but one flesh,
> and you teach us that what you have united
> may never be divided.
> Father, you have made the union of man and wife
>   so holy a mystery
> that it symbolizes marriage of Christ and his Church.
> Father, by your plan man and woman are united,
> and married life has been established
> as the one blessing that was not forfeited by
>   original sin
> or washed away in the flood.

Look with love upon this woman, your daughter,
now joined to her husband in marriage.
She asks your blessing.
Give her the grace of love and peace.
May she always follow the example of the holy
    women
whose praises are sung in the scriptures.

May her husband put his trust in her
and recognize that she is his equal
and the heir with him to the life of grace.
May he always honor her and love her
as Christ loves his bride, the Church.

Father, keep them always true to your command-
    ments.
Keep them faithful in marriage
and let them be living examples of Christian life.

Give them the strength which comes from the
    gospel
so that they may be witnesses of Christ to others.
(Bless them with children and help them to be
    good parents.
May they live to see their children's children.)
And, after a happy old age,
grant them fullness of life with the saints
in the kingdom of heaven.
We ask this through Christ our Lord.

R. Amen.

II.

Let us pray to the Lord for N. and N.
who come to God's altar at the beginning of their
    married life
so that they may always be united in love for each
    other
(as now they share in the body and blood of
    Christ).

All pray silently for a short while. Then the priest extends
his hands and continues:

Holy Father, you created mankind in your own
    image
and made man and woman to be joined as
    husband and wife
in union of body and heart
and so fulfill their mission in this world.

Father, to reveal the plan of your love,
you made the union of husband and wife
an image of the covenant between you and your
    people.
In the fulfillment of this sacrament,
the marriage of Christian man and woman
is a sign of the marriage between Christ and the
    Church.

Father, stretch out your hand, and bless N. and N.

Lord, grant that as they begin to live this sacrament
they may share with each other the gifts of your
    love

and become one in heart and mind
as witnesses to your presence in their marriage.
Help them to create a home together
(and give them children to be formed by the gospel
and to have a place in your family).

Give your blessings to N., your daughter,
so that she may be a good wife (and mother),
caring for the home,
faithful in love for her husband,
generous and kind.
Give your blessings to N., your son,
so that he may be a faithful husband
(and a good father).
Father, grant that as they come together to your
      table on earth,
so they may one day have the joy of sharing your
      feast in heaven.
We ask this through Christ our Lord.

R. Amen.

III.

My dear friends, let us ask God
for his continued blessings upon this bridegroom
      and his bride (or N. and N.).

All pray silently for a short while. Then the priest extends
his hands and continues:

Holy Father, creator of the universe,
maker of man and woman in your own likeness,
source of blessing for married life,

we humbly pray to you for this woman
who today is united with her husband in this
   sacrament of marriage.

May your fullest blessing come upon her and her
   husband
so that they may together rejoice in your gift of
   married love
(and enrich your Church with their children).

Lord, may they both praise you when they are
   happy
and turn to you in their sorrows.
May they be glad that you help them in their work
and know that you are with them in their need.
May they pray to you in the community of the
   Church,
and be your witnesses in the world.
May they reach old age in the company of their
   friends,
and come at last to the kingdom of heaven.
We ask this through Christ our Lord.

R. Amen.

PRAYERS AFTER COMMUNION

Lord,
in your love
you have given us this eucharist
to unite us with one another and with you.
As you have made N. and N.
one in this sacrament of marriage

(and in the sharing of the one bread and the one
   cup),
so now make them one in love for each other.
We ask this through Christ our Lord.

Or:

Lord,
we who have shared the food of your table
pray for our friends N. and N.,
whom you have joined together in marriage.
Keep them close to you always.
May their love for each other
proclaim to all the world
their faith in you.
We ask this through Christ our Lord.

Or:

Almighty God,
may the sacrifice we have offered
and the eucharist we have shared
strengthen the love of N. and N.,
and give us all your fatherly aid.
We ask this through Christ our Lord.

BLESSING AT THE END OF MASS

God the eternal Father keep you in love with each
   other,
so that the peace of Christ may stay with you
and be always in your home.

R. Amen.

May (your children bless you,)
your friends console you
and all men live in peace with you.

R. Amen.

May you always bear witness to the love of God in
    this world
so that the afflicted and the needy
will find in you generous friends,
and welcome you into the joys of heaven.

R. Amen.

And may almighty God bless you all,
the Father, and the Son, ✠ and the Holy Spirit.

R. Amen.

Or:

May God, the almighty Father,
give you his joy
and bless you (in your children).

R. Amen.

May the only Son of God have mercy on you
and help you in good times and in bad.

R. Amen.

May the Holy Spirit of God
always fill your hearts with his love.

R. Amen.

And may almighty God bless you all,
the Father, and the Son, and the Holy Spirit.

R. Amen.

Or:

May the Lord Jesus, who was a guest at the
wedding in Cana,
bless you and your families and friends.

R. Amen.

May Jesus, who loved his Church to the end,
always fill your hearts with his love.

R. Amen.

May he grant that, as you believe in his resurrection,
so you may wait for him in joy and hope.

R. Amen.

And may almighty God bless you all,
the Father, and the Son, ✠ and the Holy Spirit.

R. Amen.

Selecting the Readings

Read all of the scripture passages reprinted in this section that are appointed for use at the wedding liturgy. Read the comments provided. Discuss your favorites and give your reasons one to another. Also point out to one another those ideas you consider alien or difficult, remembering that Jesus often speaks to his church about things we choose not to hear in ways we consider hard to follow. Then consider that the scriptures are not a supermarket where you choose what you like while leaving the rest on the shelves. All of scripture is for our consideration and helps to form us as it has formed the church and our ancestors in faith these past two thousands years.

As you read these scriptures and consider their significance, you do well to rejoice in being part of something far bigger than yourselves. These insights, commands, gentle suggestions, and stories are what will make God part of your union, and your love the very presence on earth in tangible and visible ways of the perfecting love of God.

There are many translations of the Bible available today. Because familiarity helps us grow in our appreciation of the word of God, the translation printed here is the same one used in the Catholic churches in the United States.

READINGS FROM THE OLD TESTAMENT

1

Male and female he created them.

In the creation of humankind and in the command to multiply and fill the earth, God invites men and women to be cocreators with him in building the earthly city. In accepting the invitation, you participate in a form of love that stretches back to the beginning of time and through you stretches into the future.

A reading from the Book of Genesis   1:26–28, 31a

Then God said:
"Let us make man in our image, after our likeness.
Let them have dominion over the fish of the sea,
        the birds of the air, and the cattle,
        and over all the wild animals
        and all the creatures that crawl on the ground."

God created man in his image;
        in the image of God he created him;
        male and female he created them.

God blessed them, saying:
        "Be fertile and multiply;
        fill the earth and subdue it.
Have dominion over the fish of the sea, the birds of the air,
        and all the living things that move on the earth."

God looked at everything he had made, and he found it
very good.

The word of the Lord.

2

The two of them become one body.

*Eve is created from the side of Adam. Because man and
woman are created from the same stuff, they are equal in status
and dignity.*

*In managing the peaceable kingdom, the first man needed
help. Head of the household is still a big job for one person to
handle alone. Husband and wife, with different talents and inter-
ests, complement each other and together meet the challenges of
family life.*

A reading from the Book of Genesis   2:18–24

The LORD God said: "It is not good for the man to be alone.
I will make a suitable partner for him."
So the LORD God formed out of the ground
    various wild animals and various birds of the air,
    and he brought them to the man to see what he
      would call them;
    whatever the man called each of them would be its
      name.
The man gave names to all the cattle,
    all the birds of the air, and all wild animals;
    but none proved to be the suitable partner for
      the man.

So the LORD God cast a deep sleep on the man,
>   and while he was asleep,
>   >   he took out one of his ribs and closed up its place
>   >   >   with flesh.
The LORD God then built up into a woman the rib
>   that he had taken from the man.
When he brought her to the man, the man said:

>   "This one, at last, is bone of my bones
>   >   and flesh of my flesh;
>   This one shall be called 'woman,'
>   >   for out of 'her man' this one has been taken."

That is why a man leaves his father and mother
>   and clings to his wife,
>   and the two of them become one body.

The word of the Lord.

3

In his love for Rebekah, Isaac found solace after the death of his mother.

In this reading, Isaac and Rebekah give themselves freely, one to another, in marriage.

Marriage vows, like baptismal and confirmation promises, are usually spoken at a time when those involved cannot possibly realize the extent of what will be required of them as Christian people. Engaged couples often ask married people which years are the hardest. Any couple who gets past the first anniversary knows that the years are easy but the days are tough. If you plan to live another forty years, "all the days of your life" add up to at least 14,610 days. Like Rebekah and Isaac, you dedicate yourselves to each other with innocent faithfulness and boundless love.

(For more insight on this, see also the commentary for the following selection from Tobit.)

A reading from the Book of Genesis   24:48–51, 58–67

The servant of Abraham said to Laban:
"I bowed down in worship to the LORD,
>blessing the LORD, the God of my master Abraham,
>who had led me on the right road
>to obtain the daughter of my master's kinsman for
>>his son.
If, therefore, you have in mind to show true loyalty to my
>>master,
>let me know;
>but if not, let me know that, too.
I can then proceed accordingly."

Laban and his household said in reply:
>"This thing comes from the LORD;
>we can say nothing to you either for or against it.
Here is Rebekah, ready for you;
>take her with you,
>that she may become the wife of your master's son,
>as the LORD has said."

So they called Rebekah and asked her,
>"Do you wish to go with this man?"
She answered, "I do."

At this they allowed their sister Rebekah and her nurse to
> take leave,
along with Abraham's servant and his men.
Invoking a blessing on Rebekah, they said:

"Sister, may you grow
> into thousands of myriads;
And may your descendants gain possession
> of the gates of their enemies!"

Then Rebekah and her maids started out;
> they mounted their camels and followed the man.
So the servant took Rebekah and went on his way.

Meanwhile Isaac had gone from Beer-lahai-roi
> and was living in the region of the Negeb.
One day toward evening he went out...in the field,
> and as he looked around, he noticed that camels were
> approaching.
Rebekah, too, was looking about, and when she saw him,
> she alighted from her camel and asked the servant,
> "Who is the man out there, walking through the
> fields toward us?"
"That is my master," replied the servant.
Then she covered herself with her veil.

The servant recounted to Isaac all the things he had done.
Then Isaac took Rebekah into his tent;
> he married her, and thus she became his wife.
In his love for her Isaac found solace
> after the death of his mother Sarah.

The word of the Lord.

4

May the Lord of heaven prosper you both.
May he grant you mercy and peace.

No matter how well you think you know each other, you are strangers in many ways as you commit yourselves to the lifelong marriage relationship. You marry a young man or woman. Each of you carries "baggage" from your past—and neither one of you may realize just how heavy those bags are. And years from now, you'll both have changed, and it may not necessarily "feel like" a change for the better. You'll find yourself married to a mother, a father, a grandparent, a person with a different career, a person on unemployment, a retired person, a sick person. This reading and the preceding selection from Genesis illustrate the enormous faith you place in one another and in the awesome power of your love.

A reading from the Book of Tobit   7:6–14

Raphael and Tobiah entered the house of Raguel and
          greeted him.
Raguel sprang up and kissed Tobiah, shedding tears of joy.
But when he heard that Tobit had lost his eyesight,
          he was grieved and wept aloud.
He said to Tobiah:
          "My child, God bless you!
You are the son of a noble and good father.
But what a terrible misfortune
          that such a righteous and charitable man
          should be afflicted with blindness!"

He continued to weep in the arms of his kinsman Tobiah.
His wife Edna also wept for Tobit;
    and even their daughter Sarah began to weep.

Afterward, Raguel slaughtered a ram from the flock
    and gave them a cordial reception.
When they had bathed and reclined to eat,
    Tobiah said to Raphael, "Brother Azariah,
    ask Raguel to let me marry my kinswoman Sarah."
Raguel overheard the words;
    so he said to the boy:
    "Eat and drink and be merry tonight,
    for no man is more entitled to marry my daughter
      Sarah
    than you, brother.
Besides, not even I have the right to give her to anyone
      but you,
    because you are my closest relative.
But I will explain the situation to you very frankly.
I have given her in marriage to seven men,
    all of whom were kinsmen of ours,
    and all died on the very night they approached her.
But now, son, eat and drink.
I am sure the Lord will look after you both."
Tobiah answered, "I will eat or drink nothing
    until you set aside what belongs to me."

Raguel said to him: "I will do it.
She is yours according to the decree of the Book of Moses.
Your marriage to her has been decided in heaven!
Take your kinswoman;
    from now on you are her love,

and she is your beloved.
She is yours today and ever after.
And tonight, son, may the Lord of heaven prosper you both.
May he grant you mercy and peace."
Then Raguel called his daughter Sarah, and she came to him.
He took her by the hand and gave her to Tobiah with the
     words:
    "Take her according to the law.
According to the decree written in the Book of Moses she
     is your wife.
Take her and bring her back safely to your father.
And may the God of heaven grant both of you peace and
     prosperity."
He then called her mother and told her to bring a scroll,
     so that he might draw up a marriage contract
     stating that he gave Sarah to Tobiah as his wife
     according to the decree of the Mosaic law.
Her mother brought the scroll,
     and he drew up the contract,
     to which they affixed their seals.
Afterward they began to eat and drink.

The word of the Lord.

5

Allow us to live together to a happy old age.

After marrying Sarah, Tobiah faces imminent death, given that her previous seven husbands each died on their wedding night. So Tobiah, with Sarah, begs God for mercy. Despite Tobiah's dire circumstances (which we hope are not your own), his moving prayer is one that could easily be on the lips of married couples today: Tobiah and Sarah praise God first, speak of God's own blessing on marriage, and then ask God for the mercy of a long life together.

A reading from the Book of Tobit   8:4b–8

On their wedding night Tobiah arose from bed and said to
      his wife,
    "Sister, get up. Let us pray and beg our Lord
    to have mercy on us and to grant us deliverance."
Sarah got up, and they started to pray
    and beg that deliverance might be theirs.
They began with these words:

    "Blessed are you, O God of our fathers;
        praised be your name forever and ever.
    Let the heavens and all your creation
        praise you forever.
    You made Adam and you gave him his wife Eve
        to be his help and support;
        and from these two the human race descended.
    You said, 'It is not good for the man to be alone;
        let us make him a partner like himself.'
    Now, Lord, you know that I take this wife of mine
        not because of lust,
        but for a noble purpose.
Call down your mercy on me and on her,
    and allow us to live together to a happy old age."

They said together, "Amen, amen."

The word of the Lord.

6

The woman who fears the Lord is to be praised.

The Book of Proverbs presents a job description that might seem overwhelming to a new bride. Who can live up to these expectations? It is a simple formula: The good wife puts the needs of others before her own. She is a wise steward of the family resources. She does her best to remain patient, thoughtful, and kind in the face of life's many challenges. Her most precious quality is her relationship with the Lord. She is humble—her praise comes from her many works of love. And her husband should imitate her virtue!

A reading from the Book of Proverbs
31:10–13, 19–20, 30–31

When one finds a worthy wife,
    her value is far beyond pearls.
Her husband, entrusting his heart to her,
    has an unfailing prize.
She brings him good, and not evil,
    all the days of her life.
She obtains wool and flax
    and makes cloth with skillful hands.
She puts her hands to the distaff,
    and her fingers ply the spindle.
She reaches out her hands to the poor,
    and extends her arms to the needy.

Charm is deceptive and beauty fleeting;
　　the woman who fears the LORD is to be praised.
Give her a reward of her labors,
　　and let her works praise her at the city gates.

The word of the Lord.

7

Stern as death is love.

The Song of Songs, also known as the Song of Solomon and the Canticle of Canticles, is the only book from which no reading is appointed for use during the three-year cycle of Sunday readings. The reason, perhaps, is that the scriptural author freely uses sexual imagery to speak of love's ecstasy as a way in which to understand God's passion. The manner is so straightforward, the imagery so erotic, that those who selected the Sunday readings may have thought this canticle entirely too much for us, but this description of God's love is as sensual and exhilarating as Tobiah's is spiritual.

A reading from the Song of Songs

2:8–10, 14, 16a; 8:6–7a

Hark! my lover—here he comes
　　springing across the mountains,
　　leaping across the hills.
My lover is like a gazelle
　　or a young stag.
Here he stands behind our wall,
　　gazing through the windows,
　　peering through the lattices.

132

My lover speaks; he says to me,
>"Arise, my beloved, my dove, my beautiful one, and
>>come!

"O my dove in the clefts of the rock,
>in the secret recesses of the cliff,
Let me see you,
>let me hear your voice,
For your voice is sweet,
>and you are lovely."

My lover belongs to me and I to him.
He says to me:

"Set me as a seal on your heart,
>as a seal on your arm;
For stern as death is love,
>relentless as the nether world is devotion;
>its flames are a blazing fire.
Deep waters cannot quench love,
>nor floods sweep it away."

The word of the Lord.

8

Like the sun rising in the LORD's *heavens, the beauty of a virtuous wife is the radiance of her home.*

The perfect wife is described here; the perfect husband isn't. In reality, neither one exists. Anyone who sponsors an Internet search for the perfect Mr. or Ms. Right is destined for disappointment. The spouse who seeks perfection is one who, over the years, becomes sensitive to the other's needs, shares triumphs and challenges, and is willing to compromise. Life is rich and full when shared with such a spouse.

A reading from the Book of Sirach   26:1–4, 13–16

Blessed the husband of a good wife,
    twice-lengthened are his days;
A worthy wife brings joy to her husband,
    peaceful and full is his life.
A good wife is a generous gift
    bestowed upon him who fears the LORD;
Be he rich or poor, his heart is content,
    and a smile is ever on his face.

A gracious wife delights her husband,
    her thoughtfulness puts flesh on his bones;
A gift from the LORD is her governed speech,
    and her firm virtue is of surpassing worth.
Choicest of blessings is a modest wife,
    priceless her chaste soul.
A holy and decent woman adds grace upon grace;
    indeed, no price is worthy of her temperate soul.
Like the sun rising in the LORD's heavens,
    the beauty of a virtuous wife is the radiance of
        her home.

The word of the Lord.

9

I will make a new covenant with the house of Israel and the house of Judah.

The covenant that God enters into with his people is the model for the covenant of marriage. We have a hint here about why the church considers marriage a sacrament: its love reflects and makes present the enduring, perfecting love of God. Marriage spoken of as covenant suggests a heavy-duty promise. It isn't like promising to keep the beer cold or pay back a loan.

In ancient times, contracts were sealed by blood: the parties involved walked between the halves of freshly slaughtered animals, implying that should they not remain faithful to their promise, they should suffer the same fate. This gives new meaning to the question, "So what am I? Chopped liver?" Your marriage promises are not given lightly either, with little thought, or for a period of time any briefer than until death.

A reading from the Book of the Prophet Jeremiah
31:31–32a, 33–34a

The days are coming, says the LORD,
>   when I will make a new covenant with the house of
>   Israel
>   and the house of Judah.
It will not be like the covenant I made with their fathers:
>   the day I took them by the hand
>   to lead them forth from the land of Egypt.
But this is the covenant which I will make
>   with the house of Israel after those days, says the LORD.

I will place my law within them, and write it upon their
>hearts;
>I will be their God, and they shall be my people.
No longer will they have need to teach their friends and
>relatives
>how to know the LORD.
All, from least to greatest, shall know me, says the LORD.

The word of the Lord.

READINGS FROM THE NEW TESTAMENT

1

What will separate us from the love of Christ?

Nothing can separate us from the love of God.

Your marriage begins surrounded by the sung, spoken, and silent prayers of those who worship with you. You are invited to turn to God often in times of thanksgiving, sorrow, and need by tapping the limitless resource of grace available in and through prayer.

A reading from the Letter of Saint Paul to the Romans
8:31b–35, 37–39

Brothers and sisters:
If God is for us, who can be against us?
He who did not spare his own Son
>but handed him over for us all,
>>how will he not also give us everything else along
>>with him?

Who will bring a charge against God's chosen ones?
It is God who acquits us.
Who will condemn?
It is Christ Jesus who died, rather, was raised,
        who also is at the right hand of God,
        who indeed intercedes for us.
What will separate us from the love of Christ?
Will anguish, or distress, or persecution, or famine,
        or nakedness, or peril, or the sword?

No, in all these things, we conquer overwhelmingly
        through him who loved us.
For I am convinced that neither death, nor life,
        nor angels, nor principalities,
        nor present things, nor future things,
        nor powers, nor height, nor depth,
        nor any other creature will be able to separate us
        from the love of God in Christ Jesus our Lord.

The word of the Lord.

2

Offer your bodies as a living sacrifice, holy and pleasing to God.
LONG FORM

Paul charges us to let our behavior be changed by the new reality that Christ brings to the world. If you exercise your patience, humility, and sense of humor with each other, you will be better people and the world will be a better place.

Twenty-first-century America can be a harsh environment for a Christian marriage. The modern world urges self-fulfillment while Christ demands dedication to others. Christ asks for, and promises, a love that is permanent and unconditional. The modern reality is that many couples stay together as long as things "work out." Let your behavior as a Christian couple change the world rather than the other way around.

(This reflection is for the next two readings, both under number 2.)

A reading from the Letter of Saint Paul to the Romans
12:1–2, 9–18

I urge you, brothers and sisters, by the mercies of God,
    to offer your bodies as a living sacrifice,
      holy and pleasing to God, your spiritual worship.
Do not conform yourselves to this age
    but be transformed by the renewal of your mind,
    that you may discern what is the will of God,
    what is good and pleasing and perfect.

Let love be sincere;
    hate what is evil,
    hold on to what is good;
    love one another with mutual affection;
    anticipate one another in showing honor.
Do not grow slack in zeal,
    be fervent in spirit,
    serve the Lord.
Rejoice in hope,
    endure in affliction,
    persevere in prayer.

Contribute to the needs of the holy ones,
>   exercise hospitality.
Bless those who persecute you,
>   bless and do not curse them.
Rejoice with those who rejoice,
>   weep with those who weep.
Have the same regard for one another;
>   do not be haughty but associate with the lowly;
>   do not be wise in your own estimation.
Do not repay anyone evil for evil;
>   be concerned for what is noble in the sight of all.
If possible, on your part, live at peace with all.

The word of the Lord.

OR THE FOLLOWING

Offer your bodies as a living sacrifice, holy and pleasing to God.
SHORT FORM

A reading from the Letter of Saint Paul to the Romans
12:1–2, 9–13

I urge you, brothers and sisters, by the mercies of God,
>   to offer your bodies as a living sacrifice,
>   holy and pleasing to God, your spiritual worship.
Do not conform yourselves to this age
>   but be transformed by the renewal of your mind,
>   that you may discern what is the will of God,
>   what is good and pleasing and perfect.

Let love be sincere;
    hate what is evil,
    hold on to what is good;
    love one another with mutual affection;
    anticipate one another in showing honor.
Do not grow slack in zeal,
    be fervent in spirit,
    serve the Lord.
Rejoice in hope,
    endure in affliction,
    persevere in prayer.
Contribute to the needs of the holy ones,
    exercise hospitality.

The word of the Lord.

3

Welcome one another as Christ welcomed you.

Here Paul provides a clear statement of faith appropriate for those who present themselves as a Christian couple professing their vows in a Catholic church. Use the occasion of your wedding to offer praise and thanksgiving to the one God who gives life, and who redeems, guides, sustains, and comforts you on your journey as a couple.

A reading from the Letter of Saint Paul to the Romans
15:1b–3a, 5–7, 13

Brothers and sisters:
We ought to put up with the failings of the weak and not
        to please ourselves;
    let each of us please our neighbor for the good,
    for building up.
For Christ did not please himself....
May the God of endurance and encouragement
        grant you to think in harmony with one another,
        in keeping with Christ Jesus,
        that with one accord you may with one voice
        glorify the God and Father of our Lord Jesus Christ.

Welcome one another, then, as Christ welcomed you,
    for the glory of God.
May the God of hope fill you with all joy and peace in
        believing,
        so that you may abound in hope by the power of the
        Holy Spirit.

The word of the Lord.

4

Your body is a temple of the Spirit.

You probably keep your body—that is, the temple of the Holy Spirit—clean, tastefully decorated, and up to code. Now use it as the architect intended. We belong to Christ and should be aware of the dignity of our baptized bodies.

A reading from the First Letter of Saint Paul to the Corinthians
6:13c–15a, 17–20

Brothers and sisters:
The body is not for immorality, but for the Lord,
    and the Lord is for the body;
        God raised the Lord and will also raise us by his
           power.

Do you not know that your bodies are members of Christ?
Whoever is joined to the Lord becomes one spirit with him.
Avoid immorality.
Every other sin a person commits is outside the body,
    but the immoral person sins against his own body.
Do you not know that your body
    is a temple of the Holy Spirit within you,
        whom you have from God, and that you are not your
           own?
For you have been purchased at a price.
Therefore glorify God in your body.

The word of the Lord.

5

If I do not have love, I gain nothing.

In this, the most popular of all wedding readings, Paul describes the look and feel of love. The only ones who tire of this reading are probably priests who preside at more than fifty weddings a year.

A reading from the First Letter of Saint Paul to the Corinthians
12:31—13:8a

Brothers and sisters:
Strive eagerly for the greatest spiritual gifts.

But I shall show you a still more excellent way.

If I speak in human and angelic tongues
    but do not have love,
    I am a resounding gong or a clashing cymbal.
And if I have the gift of prophecy
    and comprehend all mysteries and all knowledge;
    if I have all faith so as to move mountains,
    but do not have love, I am nothing.
If I give away everything I own,
    and if I hand my body over so that I may boast
    but do not have love, I gain nothing.

Love is patient, love is kind.
It is not jealous, is not pompous,
    it is not inflated, it is not rude,
    it does not seek its own interests,
    it is not quick-tempered, it does not brood over
        injury, it does not rejoice over wrongdoing
    but rejoices with the truth.
It bears all things, believes all things,
    hopes all things, endures all things.

Love never fails.

The word of the Lord.

6

This is a great mystery, but I speak in reference to Christ and the church.

LONG FORM

Paul always gets a bad rap for the following reading because it is often not read carefully, and in its proper context and its entirety. He does not describe marriage as it ought to exist in every age, but uses the model of marriage that he knew. In other words, he develops the radical notion—radical for almost two-thousand years ago—that husbands and wives ought to treat each other with love and not as property. Paul takes Christ's revolutionary directive (*Love others as you love yourself*) and makes it even more revolutionary by suggesting that "others" include wives. He uses the model of Christ's love for his bride the church, and suggests that human love mirrors the perfect love of God. This reading is a must for feminists of either gender.

(*This reflection is for the next two readings, both under the number 6.*)

A reading from the Letter of Saint Paul to the Ephesians
5:2a, 21–33

Brothers and sisters:
Live in love, as Christ loved us
    and handed himself over for us.

Be subordinate to one another out of reverence for Christ.
Wives should be subordinate to their husbands as to the
    Lord.

For the husband is head of his wife
> just as Christ is head of the church,
> he himself the savior of the body.

As the church is subordinate to Christ,
> so wives should be subordinate to their husbands in
> everything.

Husbands, love your wives,
> even as Christ loved the church
> and handed himself over for her to sanctify her,
> cleansing her by the bath of water with the word,
> that he might present to himself the church in splendor,
> without spot or wrinkle or any such thing,
> that she might be holy and without blemish.

So also husbands should love their wives as their own
> bodies.

He who loves his wife loves himself.

For no one hates his own flesh
> but rather nourishes and cherishes it,
> even as Christ does the church,
> because we are members of his body.

> *For this reason a man shall leave his father and his mother*
> *and be joined to his wife,*
> *and the two shall become one flesh.*

This is a great mystery,
> but I speak in reference to Christ and the church.

In any case, each one of you should love his wife as
> himself,
> and the wife should respect her husband.

The word of the Lord.

OR THE FOLLOWING

This is a great mystery, but I speak in reference to Christ and the church.

SHORT FORM

A reading from the Letter of Saint Paul to the Ephesians
5:2a, 25–32

Brothers and sisters:
Live in love, as Christ loved us
    and handed himself over for us.

Husbands, love your wives,
    even as Christ loved the church
    and handed himself over for her to sanctify her,
    cleansing her by the bath of water with the word,
    that he might present to himself the church in splendor,
    without spot or wrinkle or any such thing,
    that she might be holy and without blemish.
So also husbands should love their wives as their own
    bodies.
He who loves his wife loves himself.
For no one hates his own flesh
    but rather nourishes and cherishes it,
    even as Christ does the church,
    because we are members of his body.

For this reason a man shall leave his father and his mother
and be joined to his wife,
and the two shall become one flesh.

This is a great mystery,
> but I speak in reference to Christ and the church.

The word of the Lord.

7

The God of peace will be with you.

"Make your requests known to God."

If you are not yet praying together as a couple, this is the time to start. Before you each go to work, put your arms around each other and say, "Lord, thank you for the gift of each other and please bless our plans for this day." Offer a simple grace before all the meals you share. And before you kiss each other goodnight, say "Thank you, God, for being with us today. Please give us the grace to do your will." These simple beginnings will make it easier for you to share your prayers with God and each other in times of great joy or great need.

A reading from the Letter of Saint Paul to the Philippians
4:4–9

Brothers and sisters:
Rejoice in the Lord always.
I shall say it again: rejoice!
Your kindness should be known to all.
The Lord is near.
Have no anxiety at all, but in everything,
> by prayer and petition, with thanksgiving,
> make your requests known to God.

Then the peace of God that surpasses all understanding
will guard your hearts and minds in Christ Jesus.

Finally, brothers and sisters,
whatever is true, whatever is honorable,
whatever is just, whatever is pure,
whatever is lovely, whatever is gracious,
if there is any excellence
and if there is anything worthy of praise,
think about these things.
Keep on doing what you have learned and received
and heard and seen in me.
Then the God of peace will be with you.

The word of the Lord.

8

And over all these put on love,
that is, the bond of perfection.

*Paul emphasizes the dignity that is each Christian's by
virtue of baptism. He tells God's chosen people how we ought to
live. The tentmaker in Paul sees things in terms of cloth; he suggests that over our other clothes, we put on the garment of love.
God's blessing on your union is not duty-free. Paul tells God's
chosen people how they ought to treat each other: with compassion, kindness, humility, gentleness, patience, forgiveness, wisdom, and gratitude. This may be difficult when your partner is
three hours late and hasn't called, or you're stuck on the side of
a four-lane highway in a car that was supposed to have a full
tank of gas—but try to remember.*

A reading from the Letter of Saint Paul to the Colossians
3:12–17

Brothers and sisters:
Put on, as God's chosen ones, holy and beloved,
   heartfelt compassion, kindness, humility, gentleness,
      and patience,
   bearing with one another and forgiving one another,
   if one has a grievance against another;
   as the Lord has forgiven you, so must you also do.
And over all these put on love,
   that is, the bond of perfection.
And let the peace of Christ control your hearts,
   the peace into which you were also called in one body.
And be thankful.
Let the word of Christ dwell in you richly,
   as in all wisdom you teach and admonish one another,
   singing psalms, hymns, and spiritual songs
   with gratitude in your hearts to God.
And whatever you do, in word or in deed,
   do everything in the name of the Lord Jesus,
   giving thanks to God the Father through him.

The word of the Lord.

9

Let marriage be held in honor by all.

Married love is not merely a matter of looking lovingly at one another. Your vows call you to look lovingly toward others as well. God has given you an incredible blessing in the love you have for each other. Take time to decide how the two of you will then become a blessing to others. Be confident of all decisions that you have considered together in prayer. The author of Hebrews reminds us what the scriptures teach over and over: If God is with us, there is nothing to fear.

A reading from the Letter to the Hebrews 13:1–4a, 5–6b

Brothers and sisters:
Let mutual love continue.
Do not neglect hospitality,
> for through it some have unknowingly entertained
> > angels.
Be mindful of prisoners as if sharing their imprisonment,
> and of the ill-treated as of yourselves,
> > for you also are in the body.
Let marriage be honored among all
> and the marriage bed be kept undefiled.
Let your life be free from love of money
> but be content with what you have,
> > for he has said, *I will never forsake you or abandon you.*
Thus we may say with confidence:

> *The Lord is my helper,*
> *and I will not be afraid.*

The word of the Lord.

10

Be of one mind, sympathetic, loving toward one another.

Here the scriptural author points out that wives can win their husbands over to the truth by their own proper behavior. The assumption is that wives have more deeply been formed by the word of God, while the men may backslide. Husbands, in turn, are admonished to treat their wives with consideration. This admonition must have been shocking to the ears of husbands who believed, as society at that time taught them, that they owned their wives.

A reading from the First Letter of Saint Peter   3:1–9

Beloved:
You wives should be subordinate to your husbands so that,
    even if some disobey the word,
        they may be won over without a word by their wives'
           conduct
    when they observe your reverent and chaste behavior.
Your adornment should not be an external one:
    braiding the hair, wearing gold jewelry, or dressing in
        fine clothes,
    but rather the hidden character of the heart,
    expressed in the imperishable beauty
    of a gentle and calm disposition,
    which is precious in the sight of God.
For this is also how the holy women who hoped in God
    once used to adorn themselves

and were subordinate to their husbands;
thus Sarah obeyed Abraham, calling him "lord."
You are her children when you do what is good
and fear no intimidation.

Likewise, you husbands should live with your wives in
understanding,
showing honor to the weaker female sex,
since we are joint heirs of the gift of life,
so that your prayers may not be hindered.

Finally, all of you, be of one mind, sympathetic,
loving toward one another, compassionate, humble.
Do not return evil for evil, or insult for insult;
but, on the contrary, a blessing, because to this you
were called,
that you might inherit a blessing.

The word of the Lord.

11

Love in deed and in truth.

*Love proves itself not through speech but action. Life with
Christ is not a destination at which we arrive but a way of trav-
eling. God wisely sees to it that we receive the guidance we need
for this challenging journey. We are guided by his commandments and by the presence of the Holy Spirit in our lives.*

A reading from the First Letter of Saint John   3:18–24

Children, let us love not in word or speech
but in deed and truth.

Now this is how we shall know that we belong to the truth
    and reassure our hearts before him
    in whatever our hearts condemn,
    for God is greater than our hearts and knows
      everything.
Beloved, if our hearts do not condemn us,
    we have confidence in God
    and receive from him whatever we ask,
    because we keep his commandments and do what
      pleases him.
And his commandment is this:
    we should believe in the name of his Son, Jesus Christ,
    and love one another just as he commanded us.
Those who keep his commandments remain in him, and
      he in them,
    and the way we know that he remains in us
    is from the Spirit that he gave us.

The word of the Lord.

12

God is love.

God has loved us first—before we even knew him, before we were ever born. We, therefore, ought to love one another. There are times in our lives when we feel so angry or hurt or powerless that we don't feel God's presence in our lives. But even when God seems so distant, he is present in the love we share with others.

A reading from the First Letter of Saint John   4:7–12

Beloved, let us love one another,
    because love is of God;
    everyone who loves is begotten by God and knows
        God.
Whoever is without love does not know God, for God is
        love.
In this way the love of God was revealed to us:
God sent his only-begotten Son into the world
    so that we might have life through him.
In this is love:
    not that we have loved God, but that he loved us
    and sent his Son as expiation for our sins.
Beloved, if God so loved us,
    we also must love one another.
No one has ever seen God.
Yet, if we love one another, God remains in us,
    and his love is brought to perfection in us.

The word of the Lord.

13

Blessed are those who have been called to the wedding feast of the Lamb.

In this reading, John compares heaven to a wedding feast. Like the bride's white linen that is made of the good deeds of the saints, your own wedding day is dazzling because of the thoughtful efforts of many loving friends and family members. Take time often to remember and pray for the people whose love and concern is woven into the fabric of your lives.

A reading from the Book of Revelation   19:1, 5–9a

I, John, heard what sounded like the loud voice
    of a great multitude in heaven, saying:
        "Alleluia!
    Salvation, glory, and might belong to our God."

A voice coming from the throne said:

    "Praise our God, all you his servants,
        and you who revere him, small and great."

Then I heard something like the sound of a great multitude
    or the sound of rushing water or mighty peals of
        thunder, as they said:
        "Alleluia!
    The Lord has established his reign,
        our God, the almighty.
    Let us rejoice and be glad
        and give him glory.
    For the wedding day of the Lamb has come,
        his bride has made herself ready.
    She was allowed to wear
        a bright, clean linen garment."

Then the angel said to me,
    "Write this:
    Blessed are those who have been called
    to the wedding feast of the Lamb."

The word of the Lord.

RESPONSORIAL PSALMS

1

33:12 and 18, 20–21, 22

R: The earth is full of the goodness of the Lord. (33:5b)

Blessed the nation whose God is the LORD,
    the people he has chosen for his own inheritance.
But see, the eyes of the LORD are upon those who fear him,
    upon those who hope for his kindness.

R: The earth is full of the goodness of the Lord.

Our soul waits for the LORD,
    who is our help and our shield,
For in him our hearts rejoice;
    in his holy name we trust.

R: The earth is full of the goodness of the Lord.

May your kindness, O LORD, be upon us
    who have put our hope in you.

R: The earth is full of the goodness of the Lord.

2

34:2–3, 4–5, 6–7, 8–9

R: I will bless the Lord at all times. (34:2a)

OR:

R: Taste and see the goodness of the Lord. (34:9a)

I will bless the LORD at all times;
    his praise shall be ever in my mouth.
Let my soul glory in the LORD;
    the lowly will hear me and be glad.

R: I will bless the Lord at all times.

OR:

R: Taste and see the goodness of the Lord.

Glorify the LORD with me,
    let us together extol his name.
I sought the LORD, and he answered me
    and delivered me from all my fears.

R: I will bless the Lord at all times.

OR:

R: Taste and see the goodness of the Lord.

Look to him that you may be radiant with joy,
    and your faces may not blush with shame.

When the poor one called out, the LORD heard,
    and from all his distress he saved him.

R: I will bless the Lord at all times.

    OR:

R: Taste and see the goodness of the Lord.

The angel of the LORD encamps
    around those who fear him, and delivers them.
Taste and see how good the LORD is;
    blessed the man who takes refuge in him.

R: I will bless the Lord at all times.

    OR:

R: Taste and see the goodness of the Lord.

3

103:1–2, 8 and 13, 17–18a

R: The Lord is kind and merciful. (103:8a)

    OR:

R: The Lord's kindness is everlasting to those who fear
    him. (See 103:17)

Bless the LORD, O my soul;
    and all my being, bless his holy name.
Bless the LORD, O my soul,
    and forget not all his benefits.

R: The Lord is kind and merciful.

OR:

R: The Lord's kindness is everlasting to those who fear him.

Merciful and gracious is the LORD,
　　slow to anger and abounding in kindness.
As a father has compassion on his children,
　　so the LORD has compassion on those who fear him.

R: The Lord is kind and merciful.

OR:

R: The Lord's kindness is everlasting to those who fear him.

But the kindness of the LORD is from eternity
　　to eternity toward those who fear him,
And his justice towards children's children
　　among those who keep his covenant.

R: The Lord is kind and merciful.

OR:

R: The Lord's kindness is everlasting to those who fear him.

4

112:1bc–2, 3–4, 5–7a, 7b–8, 9

R: Blessed the man who greatly delights in the Lord's commands. (See 112:1)

OR:

R: Alleluia.

Blessed the man who fears the LORD,
    who greatly delights in his commands.
His posterity shall be mighty upon the earth;
    the upright generation shall be blessed.

R: Blessed the man who greatly delights in the Lord's commands.

    OR:

R: Alleluia.

Wealth and riches shall be in his house;
    his generosity shall endure forever.
Light shines through the darkness for the upright;
    he is gracious and merciful and just.

R: Blessed the man who greatly delights in the Lord's commands.

    OR:

R: Alleluia.

Well for the man who is gracious and lends,
    who conducts his affairs with justice;
He shall never be moved;
    the just one shall be in everlasting remembrance.
An evil report he shall not fear.

R: Blessed the man who greatly delights in the Lord's commands.

OR:

R: Alleluia.

His heart is firm, trusting in the LORD.
His heart is steadfast; he shall not fear
      till he looks down upon his foes.

R: Blessed the man who greatly delights in the Lord's commands.

OR:

R: Alleluia.

Lavishly he gives to the poor;
      his generosity shall endure forever;
      his horn shall be exalted in glory.

R: Blessed the man who greatly delights in the Lord's commands.

OR:

R: Alleluia.

5

128:1–2, 3, 4–5

R: Blessed are those who fear the Lord. (See 128:1a)

OR:

R: See how the Lord blesses those who fear him. (128:4)

Blessed are you who fear the LORD,
    who walk in his ways!
For you shall eat the fruit of your handiwork;
    blessed shall you be, and favored.

R: Blessed are those who fear the Lord.

    OR:

R: See how the Lord blesses those who fear him.

Your wife shall be like a fruitful vine
    in the recesses of your home;
Your children like olive plants
    around your table.

R: Blessed are those who fear the Lord.

    OR:

R: See how the Lord blesses those who fear him.

Behold, thus is the man blessed
    who fears the LORD.
The LORD bless you from Zion:
    may you see the prosperity of Jerusalem
    all the days of your life.

R: Blessed are those who fear the Lord.

    OR:

R: See how the Lord blesses those who fear him.

6

145:8–9, 10 and 15, 17–18

R: The Lord is compassionate toward all his works. (145:9a)

The LORD is gracious and merciful,
    slow to anger and of great kindness.
The LORD is good to all
    and compassionate toward all his works.

R: The Lord is compassionate toward all his works.

Let all your works give you thanks, O LORD,
    and let your faithful ones bless you.
The eyes of all look hopefully to you
    and you give them their food in due season.

R: The Lord is compassionate toward all his works.

The LORD is just in all his ways
    and holy in all his works.
The LORD is near to all who call upon him,
    to all who call upon him in truth.

R: The Lord is compassionate toward all his works.

7

148:1–2, 3–4, 9–10, 11–13a, 13c–14a

R: Let all praise the name of the Lord. (148:13a)

OR:

R: Alleluia.

Alleluia.
Praise the LORD from the heavens,
    praise him in the heights;
Praise him, all you his angels,
    praise him, all you his hosts.

R: Let all praise the name of the Lord.

OR:

R: Alleluia.

Praise him, sun and moon;
    praise him, all you shining stars.
Praise him, you highest heavens,
    and you waters above the heavens.

R: Let all praise the name of the Lord.

OR:

R: Alleluia.

You mountains and all you hills,
    you fruit trees and all you cedars;

You wild beasts and all tame animals,
    you creeping things and winged fowl.

R: Let all praise the name of the Lord.

    OR:

R: Alleluia.

Let the kings of the earth and all peoples,
    the princes and all the judges of the earth,
Young men too, and maidens,
    old men and boys,
Praise the name of the Lord,
    for his name alone is exalted.

R: Let all praise the name of the Lord.

    OR:

R: Alleluia.

His majesty is above earth and heaven,
    and he has lifted his horn above the people.

R: Let all praise the name of the Lord.

    OR:

R: Alleluia.

ALLELUIA VERSE AND VERSE BEFORE THE GOSPEL

1

1 John 4:7b

Everyone who loves is begotten of God and knows God.

2

1 John 4:8b, 11

God is love.
If God loved us, we also must love one another.

3

1 John 4:12

If we love one another,
God remains in us
and his love is brought to perfection in us.

4

1 John 4:16

Whoever remains in love,
remains in God and God in him.

GOSPEL READINGS

1

Rejoice and be glad, for your reward will be great in heaven.

With the crowds in the distance, Jesus addresses his disciples, who gather around him. In that time, prosperity was believed to indicate a person's goodness, and poverty a person's wickedness. So imagine how Jesus' words, when he preached the Beatitudes, must have shocked his audience. Contrary to beliefs, he says that God's blessings are to be found in places where we might not first look.

In the day-to-day grind of family life, it is common for us to feel that we're really not doing much to advance the kingdom of God. But Christ, who can be demanding, also speaks gently to us. Happy are they who resolve quarrels at home or in the office. Happy are they who do without a dinner and a movie in order to increase their contribution to the food shelf. Happy are they who put up with resistance and complaints as they impose limits on their children. The Beatitudes give us the agenda for the reign of God; that agenda also fuels the sacramental marriage, which has both a private face and a public significance.

A reading from the holy Gospel according to Matthew
5:1–12a

When Jesus saw the crowds, he went up the mountain,
    and after he had sat down, his disciples came to him.
He began to teach them, saying:

"Blessed are the poor in spirit,
   for theirs is the kingdom of heaven.
Blessed are they who mourn,
   for they will be comforted.
Blessed are the meek,
   for they will inherit the land.
Blessed are they who hunger and thirst for
      righteousness,
   for they will be satisfied.
Blessed are the merciful,
   for they will be shown mercy.
Blessed are the clean of heart,
   for they will see God.
Blessed are the peacemakers,
   for they will be called children of God.
Blessed are they who are persecuted for the sake of
      righteousness,
   for theirs is the kingdom of heaven.
Blessed are you when they insult you and persecute you
   and utter every kind of evil against you falsely
      because of me.
Rejoice and be glad,
   for your reward will be great in heaven."

The Gospel of the Lord.

2

You are the light of the world.

Salt and light, without which life would be insipid and impossible, are compared to those faithful people who hear and put into practice the word of God. Continuing the flurry of images, the reading also says that the faithful are called to be the light of the world. The challenge to those being married is clear. Recognize, rejoice, and take pride in each other's success, accomplishments, and good deeds.

A reading from the holy Gospel according to Matthew
5:13–16

Jesus said to his disciples:
You are the salt of the earth.
But if salt loses its taste, with what can it be seasoned?
It is no longer good for anything
      but to be thrown out and trampled underfoot.
You are the light of the world.
A city set on a mountain cannot be hidden.
Nor do they light a lamp and then put it under a bushel
      basket;
      it is set on a lampstand,
      where it gives light to all in the house.
Just so, your light must shine before others,
      that they may see your good deeds
      and glorify your heavenly Father.

The Gospel of the Lord.

3

A wise man built his house on rock.
LONG FORM

Marriages, like houses, must be built on firm foundations.

Like a house, a marriage may settle from time to time. But if its foundation is firm, it will actually be secured and strengthened whenever your love for each other is expressed. Even simple, sincere words build up a marriage, like "I'm sorry," "Thank you," and "Gee, you look nice!"

(This reflection is for the next two readings, both under number 3.)

A reading from the holy Gospel according to Matthew
7:21, 24–29

Jesus said to his disciples:
"Not everyone who says to me, 'Lord, Lord,'
    will enter the kingdom of heaven,
        but only the one who does the will of my Father in
        heaven.

"Everyone who listens to these words of mine and acts on
        them
    will be like a wise man who built his house on rock.
The rain fell, the floods came,
    and the winds blew and buffeted the house.
But it did not collapse; it had been set solidly on rock.
And everyone who listens to these words of mine
        but does not act on them
    will be like a fool who built his house on sand.

The rain fell, the floods came,
>   and the winds blew and buffeted the house.
And it collapsed and was completely ruined."

When Jesus finished these words,
>   the crowds were astonished at his teaching,
>   for he taught them as one having authority,
>   and not as their scribes.

The Gospel of the Lord.

OR THE FOLLOWING

A wise man built his house on rock.
SHORT FORM

A reading from the holy Gospel according to Matthew
7:21, 24–25

Jesus said to his disciples:
"Not everyone who says to me, 'Lord, Lord,'
>   will enter the kingdom of heaven,
>   but only the one who does the will of my Father in
>   heaven.

"Everyone who listens to these words of mine and acts on
>   them
>   will be like a wise man who built his house on rock.
The rain fell, the floods came,
>   and the winds blew and buffeted the house.
But it did not collapse; it had been set solidly on rock."

The Gospel of the Lord.

4

What God has united, man must not separate.

Man and woman leave mother and father and cling to one another. What God has joined, no one must separate. But there is more to fidelity than just "staying" in the marriage. You must also promise to be loyal and supportive of each other, even at times that do not seem to be of earth-shaking significance.

A reading from the holy Gospel according to Matthew
19:3–6

Some Pharisees approached Jesus, and tested him, saying,
    "Is it lawful for a man to divorce his wife for any
        cause whatever?"
He said in reply, "Have you not read that from the
        beginning
    the Creator *made them male and female* and said,
    For this reason a man shall leave his father and mother
    and be joined to his wife, and the two shall become one
        flesh?
So they are no longer two, but one flesh.
Therefore, what God has joined together, man must not
        separate."

The Gospel of the Lord.

5

This is the greatest and the first commandment. The second is like it.

Which commandment is the greatest? Jesus easily answers the question that had been intended to trip him up. He also adds a second commandment to the law. Together these few verses serve as a condensed version of all the scriptures.

As simple and familiar as these two laws sound, we know that it is difficult to live as Jesus asks. Likewise, your vows, so simple in their beauty and familiarity, will change you and challenge you every day of your married life.

A reading from the holy Gospel according to Matthew
22:35–40

One of the Pharisees, a scholar of the law, tested Jesus by
> asking,
>> "Teacher, which commandment in the law is the
>> greatest?"
He said to him,
>> "You shall love the Lord, your God,
>> with all your heart,
>> with all your soul,
>> and with all your mind.
This is the greatest and the first commandment.
The second is like it:
>> You shall love your neighbor as yourself.
The whole law and the prophets depend on these two
> commandments."

The Gospel of the Lord.

6

They are no longer two, but one flesh.

"And the two shall become one flesh…" In marriage, the whole is definitely greater than the sum of the parts. Good marriages are never 50-50. Act as a team and not as scorekeepers.

A reading from the holy Gospel according to Mark
10:6–9

Jesus said:
"From the beginning of creation,
God made them male and female.
For this reason a man shall leave his father and mother
and be joined to his wife,
and the two shall become one flesh.
So they are no longer two but one flesh.
Therefore what God has joined together,
no human being must separate."

The Gospel of the Lord.

7

Jesus did this as the beginning of his signs in Cana in Galilee.

Jesus is the perfect guest: he transforms water into wine and the party continues. This is his first public miracle. Catholics see the fact that the occurrence took place at a wedding as scriptural foundation for the sacrament of marriage. Christ blesses the marriage union and through married love lets his presence be both visible and tangible to all the world.

This reading, of course, really isn't a lesson on what can happen when unexpectedly thirsty guests show up at a reception. It's a lesson about miracles and what miracles proclaim. You repeat a miracle daily as you and your spouse become sacrament with one another. As water was changed to wine, your love for each other changes ordinary people into signs and symbols of God's presence among us on earth.

A reading from the holy Gospel according to John
2:1–11

There was a wedding in Cana in Galilee,
    and the mother of Jesus was there.
Jesus and his disciples were also invited to the wedding.
When the wine ran short,
    the mother of Jesus said to him,
    "They have no wine."
And Jesus said to her,
    "Woman, how does your concern affect me?
My hour has not yet come."
His mother said to the servers,
    "Do whatever he tells you."
Now there were six stone water jars there for Jewish
        ceremonial washings,
    each holding twenty to thirty gallons.
Jesus told them,
    "Fill the jars with water."
So they filled them to the brim.
Then he told them,
    "Draw some out now and take it to the headwaiter."

So they took it.
And when the headwaiter tasted the water that had
        become wine,
    without knowing where it came from
    (although the servants who had drawn the water knew),
    the headwaiter called the bridegroom and said to him,
    "Everyone serves good wine first,
    and then when people have drunk freely, an inferior
        one;
    but you have kept the good wine until now."
Jesus did this as the beginning of his signs in Cana in
        Galilee
    and so revealed his glory,
    and his disciples began to believe in him.

The Gospel of the Lord.

8

Remain in my love.

Just as Jesus is united to the Father in love, so also are we united one to another through him to the Father. Jesus does not suggest, but rather commands, that his followers love one another just as he has loved them.

It would seem impossible for us to demonstrate our love to the extent that Jesus did. Yet, as husbands and wives, mothers and fathers, you will be thrust into many opportunities to serve others with selfless love. The daily, mundane acts of feeding, clothing, forgiving, nursing, healing, and celebrating with your loved ones continue the work begun by Christ.

A reading from the holy Gospel according to John
15:9–12

Jesus said to his disciples:
"As the Father loves me, so I also love you.
Remain in my love.
If you keep my commandments, you will remain in my love,
    just as I have kept my Father's commandments
    and remain in his love.

I have told you this so that my joy might be in you
    and your joy might be complete.
This is my commandment: love one another as I love you."

The Gospel of the Lord.

9

This is my commandment:
love one another.

Jesus reminds us that we are his friends when we do as he commands. But your relationship with God does not begin and end with the command to go to church. Neither can your love for each other be contained within the bounds of family life. Your love extends itself willingly and frequently to others.

A reading from the holy Gospel according to John
15:12–16

Jesus said to his disciples:
"This is my commandment: love one another as I love you.

No one has greater love than this,
    to lay down one's life for one's friends.
You are my friends if you do what I command you.
I no longer call you slaves,
    because a slave does not know what his master is
        doing.
I have called you friends,
    because I have told you everything I have heard from
        my Father.
It was not you who chose me, but I who chose you
    and appointed you to go and bear fruit that will remain,
    so that whatever you ask the Father in my name he
        may give you."

The Gospel of the Lord.

10

That they may be brought to perfection as one.
LONG FORM

The love of God has existed from before the foundation of the earth. Jesus prays that we who are united in him may share always in that perfecting love.

There are many reasons for proclaiming your vows publicly in church. Whatever those reasons may be, by asking God's blessing on your union, you are making a statement about what is significant to you at this important time in your life. So think: are you reaffirming your desire to follow Christ or merely following a family tradition?

(This reflection is for the next two readings, both under the number 10.)

A reading from the holy Gospel according to John
17:20–26

Jesus raised his eyes to heaven and said:
"I pray not only for my disciples,
> but also for those who will believe in me through
> > their word,
> so that they may all be one,
> as you, Father, are in me and I in you,
> that they also may be in us,
> that the world may believe that you sent me.
And I have given them the glory you gave me,
> so that they may be one, as we are one,
> I in them and you in me,
> that they may be brought to perfection as one,
> that the world may know that you sent me,
> and that you loved them even as you loved me.
Father, they are your gift to me.
I wish that where I am they also may be with me,
> that they may see my glory that you gave me,
> because you loved me before the foundation of the
> > world.
Righteous Father, the world also does not know you,
> but I know you, and they know that you sent me.
I made known to them your name and I will make it
> > known,
> that the love with which you loved me
> may be in them and I in them."

The Gospel of the Lord.

OR THE FOLLOWING

That they may be brought to perfection as one.
SHORT FORM

A reading from the holy Gospel according to John

17:20–23

Jesus raised his eyes to heaven and said:
"Holy Father, I pray not only for these,
>but also for those who will believe in me through
>>their word,
>so that they may all be one,
>as you, Father, are in me and I in you,
>that they also may be in us,
>that the world may believe that you sent me.
And I have given them the glory you gave me,
>so that they may be one, as we are one,
>I in them and you in me,
>that they may be brought to perfection as one,
>that the world may know that you sent me,
>and that you loved them even as you loved me."

The Gospel of the Lord.

THE REHEARSAL

The Rehearsal

Beginning the wedding rehearsal is rather like handing over your ticket for a roller-coaster ride. By this time, things are pretty much out of your control. What's done is done. What isn't done probably won't get done and you'll survive the experience anyway. The rehearsal serves to smooth out some of the twists and turns of this most exhilarating ride. All of the passengers, including the priest, need to be acutely aware of the needs and concerns of others as zero hour rapidly approaches.

Punctuality, always a gesture of respect, is mandatory for both priest and wedding party alike where the rehearsal is concerned. The priest might have a meeting or another rehearsal after yours and will not be able to wait for latecomers. If you have friends who are rarely on time, simply tell them and confirm by mail or e-mail: "We will gather at the church at 5:00 p.m." You are not lying to them if the rehearsal doesn't actually begin until 5:30. If they arrive at 5:00, so much the better. They can socialize and take a tour of the church before things get underway.

The wedding party has the right to presume that the rehearsal will begin and end on time so that other festivities will stay on schedule. The rehearsal dinner should always be after your work at the church is complete.

Everyone will feel at ease if you arrive early, stand at the door, welcome each one who comes, and introduce those who haven't met. It is especially important that everyone is introduced to the priest. Start with your parents. "Father Backous, these are my parents, Stella and Stanley Kowalski, who have just arrived by streetcar from Desire. Mom and Dad, I'd like you to meet Father Backous, our pastor." They will smile, shake hands, and say to each other, "I've heard so much about you," which they may interpret any way they like. Then introduce the priest to the members of your wedding party. Even if he doesn't remember all the names, he will remember most of the connections. During the rehearsal, he would like to be able to address your maid of honor as "Meg" or "Jo's sister" or "Miss March" instead of "the one over there with the big blue eyes and the bad perm."

Most of us try to get by with introductions like this: "Scott, Julie. Julie, Scott." You will feel more confident about making new friends and keeping the old if you remember this hot little etiquette tip: It is customary to address the older person first, introducing him or her to the younger. "Grandpa, this is my best friend, Blanche DuBois. Blanche, this is my grandfather, Andrew Marvel."

At the appointed time, shepherd your loved ones into the first two pews on one side of the church, welcome them as a group, and thank them for helping to make these days so joyous. While everyone is convened and somewhat attentive in the hushed atmosphere of the church, you have the opportunity for last-minute instructions. These should include gentle reminders about keeping cell phones turned off inside the church, as well as restrictions about the wearing of baseball hats, on smoking and drinking in the church, chewing gum during the ceremony, being on time, and so on. If it helps, preface these admonitions with, "Father Backous said...."

If you would like to begin the rehearsal with a prayer, check with the priest. Otherwise he will do the honors. The wedding prayer on page v would be suitable and can be personalized to include the bride and the groom.

When you practice the vows, the priest asks, "Will you love and honor each other as husband and wife for the rest of your lives?" There is a strong temptation to slap your thigh, stamp your foot, and respond, "No," or "(long pause)...I'm thinking." Giggling may be a time-honored way of releasing tension and does not in any way predict the behavior of the giggler during the actual ceremony. It does, however, slow down the proceedings and should be kept to a minimum. Practicing your stand-up routine at the rehearsal wastes the time you need to ask the priest those questions that have plagued you and your mothers in the middle of countless nights.

The priest plays a key role in the launching of a new Christian family. A wise priest will remember that, while the wedding day may be another work day for him, it is as momentous an occasion to you as as his ordination was to him. He will see the rehearsal as an opportunity to work with a wide variety of churched and unchurched Catholics and non-Catholics. It is the perfect time for some friendly, good natured evangelization.

To folks who have had little exposure to Catholic priests, your presider is representing the church. If you have made every attempt to observe the guidelines of the parish, etiquette, and common sense, your priest is sure to temper efficiency with grace and good humor. When the rehearsal is over, everyone will be in a good mood and looking forward to the festivities.

THE AUDIENCE

Guests

Many families report that compiling a guest list for a wedding is only slightly less complicated and more stressful than filling out a federal income tax return.

The best piece of advice may be this: Do not, under any circumstances, invite anyone with the assumption that she or he will be unable to attend. As soon as you write a check to the caterer for 279 plates of beef Wellington with new potatoes and creamed onions, you will get a call from Ginny and Babs, the bride's sorority sisters, who just decided that it would be a gas to fly in from Manitoba. With their husbands.

Once the list is absolutely final, with all question marks erased, your friends will assume three different roles.

Your friends and family members are considered guests when you plan the rehearsal dinner, the reception, or any other purely social function. While thinking of them this way, you may secretly wonder what sort of gift they might choose, how much they will eat and drink, and how they will behave toward one another.

You may think of your friends as spectators when planning your wardrobe, the lineup of your attendants, and the color of the horse-drawn carriage that will transport you to the reception. There is little to worry about here. This is one audience sure to give a glowing review.

However, when planning the liturgy, you must consider that your friends are gathering in a church as worshipers, members of a congregation praying together for the first time.

When treating your friends as guests or spectators, you wouldn't dream of noticing that their religious practices might differ from your own. When thinking of your friends as worshipers, you must recognize and respect diverse backgrounds.

This would not be a problem if you exchanged vows at the 10:00 a.m. Mass on a Sunday morning. All assembled would either know the prayers or have a pretty good idea where to find them. They would also anticipate the proper responses and gestures. Drop those faithful Catholics into a Lutheran church some morning. "What? No kneelers? No sign of the cross? Our bodies just don't work this way!"

People unaccustomed to a Catholic liturgy may find themselves distracted by the thought of doing the wrong thing on your important day.

"But," the bride objects, "my family has belonged to Sts. Protect & Preserve Us ever since I was a little girl!" That might be true, but it's a safe bet that not all of your friends can make the same claim to fame.

One way to accommodate a non-Catholic bride or groom, prospective in-laws and friends is to exchange vows in a wedding liturgy that does not include a Mass.

Brides and grooms might find this adjustment quite acceptable. Concerned Catholic parents and grandparents, on the other hand, may need to be convinced by the pastor that a sacramental union is, in fact, completed with or without the Eucharist. (See "To Eucharist or Not to Eucharist?" on pages 102–3.)

Guests, spectators, and worshipers alike should be treated with utmost respect as you outline the schedule of events. If you indicate on the invitation that the wedding will begin at 11:30 a.m., the wedding should begin at 11:30 a.m. If you allow the photographer to delay you for fifteen minutes, take a long-distance call from your twin brother stationed in Peru, and then wait for all ten members of the Tuscadaro family (who are always late for everything) to sign the guest book, people will groan rather than grin as you walk down the aisle.

After the wedding, you must get to the reception as soon as possible. You're tempting fate if you spend another hour with the photographer while your guests spend that same hour at the bar. Having your pictures taken before the wedding eliminates this problem very nicely and gives you something fun to do to unwind a little bit before the liturgy begins.

If you notice the priest or the organist absent from the reception, you may have forgotten to invite them. Few people attend parties to which they have not been invited. It's too late to think of it when the food is being served, so don't ask the father of the bride or the best man to go knock on doors. During the rehearsal it is too late to invite anyone anywhere. Believe it or not, priests have social lives that go beyond wedding receptions and Knights of Columbus pancake breakfasts. Musicians have families with plans for the rest of the weekend. Be sure to invite all guests in plenty of time for them to arrange to join you.

The Receiving Line

One of the most anxiety-producing events in all of weddingdom is the receiving line. Even people who are not usually shy tend to blanch at the prospect of greeting a whole church full of people one by one.

Perhaps you have suggested to your intended that you skip the receiving line altogether because you don't want to do it and because it takes time that could be better spent partying at the reception. In your heart of hearts you know that's not right.

The task is not nearly as difficult as it first appears. Go out right now and get a Powdermilk Biscuit, which you undoubtedly have on hand from the folks in Lake Wobegon, Minnesota. This will give you the strength to do the things that need to be done. Greeting your guests individually is one of those things.

Some brides and grooms greet their guests while making the rounds at the reception. This hit-and-miss approach is chancy because you will miss as many as you hit and probably interrupt some very interesting conversations in the process.

The unavoidable fact is that you have invited all your guests because you want them to share this festive event with you. Not to greet each one of them personally is worse than a simple social gaffe, and the receiving line is the only sure way to fulfill this obligation.

The following options and suggestions will make it easier.

Though some families attempt to receive guests before the wedding, that time is usually taken up with other matters like adjusting boutonnieres and bra straps. The more traditional approach is to wait until the ceremony concludes, then line up the principals either at the door of the church or at the entrance of wherever the reception will be held.

Some families invite all members of the wedding party, parents and grandparents, aunts, uncles, and their dog Phydeaux to stand with them. This is neither practical nor necessary.

Those hosting the party, and their guests of honor, receive their guests. This means the bride and groom and their parents. Period. If there have been remarriages by any of the parents, consult those intimately involved before deciding who will greet the guests with you. Don't hesitate to ask the priest for help or advice.

Who stands where and why?

Protocol dictates that each family member will introduce friends and relatives to members of the other family. Therefore, no one in the receiving line should stand next to his or her spouse (except for the newlyweds, of course). From left to right, you should read like this: bride's mother, groom's father, bride, groom, bride's father, groom's mother. There may be slight variation if there are additional parents due to remarriage.

The supposition that each family member will introduce his or her friends is pious fiction at its best. The reality is that on a wedding day you will have enough trouble remembering your own name let alone the name of the lady who used to help your mother plant her garden every spring since you were a baby.

Simply greet each guest with a warm smile, a hug and kiss or a firm handshake, and one of the following lines: "How good to see you!" "We're so glad you could join us!" or "Thanks so much for coming!" You need remember only these three lines or reasonable facsimiles thereof. Those passing through the line will hear you say something different to each guest and your breezy self-confidence will put them at ease.

It's not quite over yet. After delivering one of the receiving lines, you then turn to the person next to you in line and say to the guest, "Have you met the father of the groom?" (or whoever it is). Isn't that great? You don't have to remember anyone's name! And it's better if you don't even try. Otherwise, you are sure to forget that your sister Pat and her new husband (also Pat) have decided to be called Trish and Patrick, and have different last names.

These tips are foolproof and should be shared with all who plan to join you in this demanding task, especially those who assume that it is more demanding than it really is.

You might also remember that there are no enemies at your wedding. These people have accepted your invitation because they want to rejoice with you on this special day. Let them come individually to say how glad they are to share in your happiness!

PART II
Behind the Scenes

How to Get the Most
Out of Marriage Prep

It is usually difficult to get married in a Catholic church without at least three months' advance notice. The time between your request and the actual ceremony is not a waiting period but a preparation period. Because Catholic tradition says that you only go around once where marriage is concerned, it is the duty of the church to see to it that you are as well prepared as possible to make this permanent commitment.

Requirements imposed by your parish or diocese are designed to be helpful, and not a series of hoops through which you must jump, gowned, veiled, and tuxed, before you may exchange vows.

Marriage prep varies in form and content depending on where you live. You might have options that range from spending an entire weekend at a retreat house to visiting with your pastor for a few hours.

No matter what type of instruction is available, the same advice you always received about every class you ever took applies here: You get out of it what you put into it.

Here are several suggestions to help make these usually mandatory sessions quite bearable.

First of all, sign up early. Second of all, sign up early. Third of all, sign up early.

If you register as soon as possible after the date is set, you will be guaranteed a spot in the program of your choice.

And you will enjoy it more. Two weeks before the wedding it is impossible to concentrate on communication, conflict resolution, and sacramental grace if the rings don't fit, the airline tickets haven't arrived, and the best man has chicken pox. If you enter into the process of preparing for marriage at least six months before the wedding, you will be able to focus on really important issues like how many Thanksgiving dinners one couple can reasonably be expected to consume in one day.

Another advantage of signing on early is that you will have more time to work on the areas of your relationship that need it. Two weeks before the wedding is not the time to find out that he wants a house filled with kids while she's thinking more along the lines of an apartment and maybe a hamster. With six or more months to go, a wedding can be discreetly delayed if it becomes apparent that there are major differences to be resolved.

Give your marriage-prep sessions high priority. Know when you are expected to arrive and how long you are expected to stay. Arrange well in advance to take off work if necessary.

Rather than just one more thing on a long list of things to do, turn it into a date and go out to eat afterward (or before if it's an evening session), either alone or with some of the other couples.

If your partner is reluctant to attend, discuss the reasons for the doubt before you go. There's nothing worse than having to go with a partner who is dead set against the idea.

If you have allowed enough time before the wedding, relax and enjoy the chance to spend some quality time together.

Avoid:

- Asking your mother to make the arrangements. You may have thought that your "accomplishments" of graduating from college, getting drunk once, and buying life insurance were sufficient notice to society of your status as an adult. Getting married tops them all, so Mom shouldn't have to do the work.
- Complaining about the cost of the program. Considering what you'll spend on flowers, pictures, and all the et ceteras, marriage preparation is cheap at twice the price.
- An unexcused no-show. Whenever you make a reservation for anything, the only acceptable excuse for not calling if you can't come is an unexpected death—yours.

RECORDS AND PAPERS AND SO ON

Catholics do lots of paperwork before they get to the altar. Some of it may seem like busy work to you. Some days it probably seems like that to your pastor, too. All of these steps, however, are taken to safeguard your individual rights and to make clear to you the seriousness of the step you are taking. It really shouldn't be any easier to get married than it is to get papers for your new puppy.

The priest will ask you to get a recently issued copy of your baptismal certificate (that means issued more recently than six months ago; the souvenir edition in your mother's cedar chest isn't the one you need). If you will be married in the church of your baptism, you can ignore this first piece of paperwork. Those to be married in a parish other than that of their baptism will find that the certificate will be supplied routinely at your request by the pastor of the parish in which you were baptized.

The flip side of the baptismal certificate will indicate that you have not been married and will then serve as a statement of your current freedom to marry. If you really want to impress the priest, arrive at your first interview with baptismal certificate in hand. Simply write or call the church of your baptism, telling them your name, your parents' names (including mom's maiden name), the date of your birth, and the approximate date of your baptism. Enclose a self-addressed and stamped envelope for speedier delivery.

Someone baptized in another Christian church may find it more difficult to get a current certificate. In this case, any proof of baptism will be acceptable.

After your marriage, the church of baptism of the Catholic party will be officially informed and notation of the marriage will be added to your baptismal record.

Catholics are among the world's best record keepers!

You can check out the sample baptismal certificate here to know what kind of document to expect.

The Holy Sacrament
of Baptism

This is to certify that _____

child of _____ and _____

born in _____(city)

_____(state)

on _____, 19_____

was Baptized on _____

in the Church of _____

City_____

according to the Roman Rite of the Catholic Church

by the Rev. _____

Sponsors were _____ and

_____

as recorded in the Baptismal Register of this church.

Pastor_____

Date_____

Notations

FIRST COMMUNION
_____

_____

CONFIRMATION
_____

_____

MARRIAGE
_____

_____

ORDINATION
_____

_____

RELIGIOUS PROFESSION
_____

_____

Affidavit Concerning Marital Freedom

If either or both of you are not known personally by the priest who is assisting you, he may ask for an Affidavit Concerning Marital Freedom. This simply means that he needs from someone who knows you well a statement that you are free to marry.

If he asks you to have the form completed, the witness (a parent, sibling, relative, friend, or associate) is asked to bring it to any Catholic priest and have him ask the necessary questions. Both the witness of your choice and the priest sign the form; it is then hit with the church's seal and is mailed or carried back to the priest who first gave it to you.

A sample of that form follows.

PRIEST ARRANGING MARRIAGE:

Name _____

Parish _____

Address _____

WITNESS TO BE INTERVIEWED:

Name _____

Parish _____

City _____

Date of Marriage: _____

AFFIDAVIT CONCERNING THE
MARITAL FREEDOM OF

_____

(Hereinafter referred to as "This Person")

Are you related to this person? _____ If so, how? _____

_____

If not, how long and how well do you know this person?

_____

_____

Has this person ever been married before (Church or civil)?
_____ (If the answer is "Yes," please give the details—
number of previous marriage(s), name of former spouse(s),
date and place of previous marriage(s), etc.)

_____

_____

Do the parents of this person approve of the forthcoming
marriage? _____
If not, what is their objection?

_____

_____

Do you know of any reason why this person should not be
married in the Catholic Church now? _____ If so, why
not? _____

_____

Do you know of anything else that should be disclosed in
regard to this person's forthcoming marriage?

_____

Do you declare that the above answers are the entire truth?

_____

SEAL _____
      (Signature of Witness)

_____
      (Signature of Priest)

_____

Date: _____

Prenuptial Interview

In addition to the basics of name, address, and dates of birth and baptism, your priest or deacon will also ask you some questions that will indicate your freedom and ability to be married. He'll tell you why he needs to know and what he must ask.

Usually, he will ask these questions of each of you individually so that you have the opportunity to say in privacy that you are entering marriage freely.

He will explain that an impediment is something that would stand in the way of your marriage. If one of you is a priest or nun, for example, you cannot enter a valid, sacramental marriage. Relation by blood is another impediment. In the unlikely event that an impediment exists, the priest will help you to understand how civil or canon law affects you.

A form similar to the one he will complete with you follows.

Prenuptial Interview: *The Groom*

NAME _____

ADDRESS _____

TELEPHONE _____

BIRTHDATE _____

Is your name as appears above that given at birth? _____

IF NOT, THE PRIEST WILL REVIEW THE DOCUMENTATION.

Parish to which you belong? _____

Father's name _____

Mother's maiden name _____

What religion do you actively profess? _____

In what religion were you baptized? _____

Confirmed? ____Yes____No

In what church were you baptized? _____

NAME AND PLACE

Date of Baptism? _____

FOR CATHOLICS INCLUDE CERTIFICATE ISSUED WITHIN PAST 6 MONTHS.

How long have you known your intended spouse? _____

When did you become engaged? _____

Do you have any doubts about entering this marriage? ____

Are you bound by any of the following impediments to marriage?

    Vows/Sacred orders (C. 1078)____Yes____ No;

    Crime (C. 1090) _____Yes____No;

    Blood Relationship (C. 1091) ____Yes____No;

    Affinity (C. 1092) _____ Yes____No;

    Public Propriety (C. 1093) _____Yes_____ No;

    Legal Relationship (C. 1094) ____Yes ____No

Are you aware of any physical or psychological condition which would hinder or interfere with your marriage.

_____

Have you ever attempted or entered a marriage previously?
IF AFFIRMATIVE, SEE BACK PAGE.
Are you placing any conditions on your marriage consent?

_____

Are you marrying because of force or fear arising from persons or circumstances? _____

Is there anything else which you should reveal concerning your proposed marriage? _____

I understand that Christian marriage is an irrevocable covenant which is both permanent and indissoluble. I also understand the responsibilities of marriage. Accordingly, I am entering this marriage freely and I intend to be faithful to my spouse.

_____   _____

SIGNATURE OF GROOM   DATE

TO BE COMPLETED BY PRIEST/DEACON:

I personally vouch for the freedom to marry of the groom.
_____ Yes _____ No
Since the groom is unknown to me, a freedom to marry affidavit is included.
_____ Yes _____ No

_____   _____

SIGNATURE OF PRIEST/DEACON   CHURCH AND PLACE

Prenuptial Interview: *The Bride*

NAME _____

ADDRESS _____

TELEPHONE _____

BIRTHDATE _____

Is your name as appears above that given at birth?_____
IF NOT, THE PRIEST WILL REVIEW THE DOCUMENTATION.

Parish to which you belong? _____

Father's name _____

Mother's maiden name _____

What religion do you actively profess? _____

In what religion were you baptized? _____

Confirmed? ____Yes____No

In what church were you baptized? _____
                                  NAME AND PLACE

Date of Baptism? _____
FOR CATHOLICS INCLUDE CERTIFICATE ISSUED WITHIN PAST 6 MONTHS.

How long have you known your intended spouse? _____

When did you become engaged? _____

Do you have any doubts about entering this marriage?_____

Are you bound by any of the following impediments to marriage?

   Vows/Sacred orders (C. 1078)____Yes____ No;

   Crime (C. 1090) ____Yes____No;

   Blood Relationship (C. 1091) ____Yes____No;

   Affinity (C. 1092) _____ Yes____No;

   Public Propriety (C. 1093) _____Yes_____ No;

   Legal Relationship (C. 1094) ____Yes ____No

Are you aware of any physical or psychological condition which would hinder or interfere with your marriage.

_____

Have you ever attempted or entered a marriage previously?
IF AFFIRMATIVE, SEE BACK PAGE.
Are you placing any conditions on your marriage consent?

_____

Are you marrying because of force or fear arising from persons or circumstances? _____
Is there anything else which you should reveal concerning your proposed marriage? _____

I understand that Christian marriage is an irrevocable covenant which is both permanent and indissoluble. I also understand the responsibilities of marriage. Accordingly, I am entering this marriage freely and I intend to be faithful to my spouse.

_____   _____
SIGNATURE OF BRIDE   DATE

TO BE COMPLETED BY PRIEST/DEACON:

I personally vouch for the freedom to marry of the bride.
_____ Yes _____ No
Since the bride is unknown to me, a freedom to marry affidavit is included.
_____ Yes _____ No

_____   _____
SIGNATURE OF PRIEST/DEACON   CHURCH AND PLACE

Some Questions When There Has Been a Former Marriage by the Prospective Bride

PREVIOUS MARRIAGES OF BRIDE

1. Name of first spouse? _____
   Religion of first spouse? _____
   When did marriage occur? _____
   Was marriage invalid? If so, why? _____
   Who officiated? (*Priest, minister, civil official?*) _____
   Is spouse still living? (*If deceased, attach certificate.*) _____
   Was marriage dissolved by divorce or by church decree? (*Attach document or decree.*) _____

2. Name of second spouse? _____
   Religion of second spouse? _____
   When did marriage occur? _____
   Was marriage invalid? If so, why? _____
   Who officiated? (*Priest, minister, civil official?*) _____
   Is spouse still living? (*If deceased, attach certificate.*) _____
   Was marriage dissolved by divorce or by church decree? (*Attach document or decree.*) _____

What obligations do you have toward any previous spouse or children from previous union?

Some Questions When There Has Been a Former Marriage by the Prospective Groom

PREVIOUS MARRIAGES OF GROOM

1. Name of first spouse? _____
   Religion of first spouse? _____
   When did marriage occur? _____
   Was marriage invalid? If so, why? _____
   Who officiated? (*Priest, minister, civil official?*) _____
   Is spouse still living? (*If deceased, attach certificate.*) _____
   Was marriage dissolved by divorce or by church
   decree? (*Attach document or decree.*) _____

2. Name of second spouse? _____
   Religion of second spouse? _____
   When did marriage occur? _____
   Was marriage invalid? If so, why? _____
   Who officiated? (*Priest, minister, civil official?*) _____
   Is spouse still living? (*If deceased, attach certificate.*) _____
   Was marriage dissolved by divorce or by church
   decree? (*Attach document or decree.*) _____

What obligations do you have toward any previous spouse
or children from previous union?

Marriage Between a Catholic and a Baptized Non-Catholic

A Catholic who will marry a baptized non-Catholic requires the permission of the Catholic bishop. This permission is routinely given for the "spiritual welfare of the parties."

A form similar to the one your priest must complete is included here.

Canonical Permission for a Marriage Between a Catholic and Baptized Non-Catholic

By virtue of the faculty granted me by the Bishop of the Diocese of _____ I hereby grant permission for the marriage between _____, a Catholic, and _____, a baptized non-Catholic, to take place on _____ at _____.

In accord with Canon 1125, the declaration and promise of the Catholic party have been given.

Canonical reasons for this permission:
____ 1. Spiritual welfare of the parties
____ 2. Well-founded hope that the non-Catholic will enter full communion with the church
____ 3. Danger of attempted invalid marriage
____ 4. Convalidation
____ 5. Other (Specify):

_____   _____
DATE   PRIEST/DEACON

                         _____
                         CHURCH

                         _____
                         CITY & STATE

Dispensation from the Impediment of Disparity of Cult

A form similar to the following one is completed when a Catholic plans a marriage to someone who is not baptized. This permission, like the last one, is readily given for the "spiritual welfare of the parties."

Dispensation from the Impediment of Disparity of Cult (*Ad Cautelam*)

Note: This form is to be used for the marriage of a Catholic and non-baptized or doubtfully baptized party.

By virtue of the faculty granted me by the Bishop of the Diocese of _____ I hereby grant a dispensation from the impediment of Disparity of Cult (*Ad Cautelam*) as it exists between _____, the Catholic party, and _____, the non-baptized or doubtfully baptized party. This marriage will take place on _____ at_____ .

In accord with Canon 1125, the declaration and promise of the Catholic party have been given.

The reason for this request is _____

_____

_____ _____
DATE   PRIEST/DEACON

            _____
            CHURCH

            _____
            CITY & STATE

Promise of the Catholic Party

In a marriage with a non-Catholic, the Catholic party must promise that children will be raised as Catholics. It should be noted that the Catholic also promises to respect "the conscience of my partner in marriage." The non-Catholic is not asked to make this promise.

A sample declaration and promise follows.

DECLARATION AND PROMISE OF THE CATHOLIC PARTY

I, _____, reaffirm my faith in Jesus Christ and, with God's help, intend to continue living that faith in the Catholic Church. At the same time, I acknowledge the respect I owe to the conscience of my partner in marriage. Therefore, I promise to do all I can to share the faith I have received with our children by having them baptized and educated as Catholics.

STATEMENT OF THE PRIEST/DEACON

The required promise and declaration have been made by the Catholic party in my presence. The non-Catholic party has been informed of this requirement so that it is certain he/she is aware of the promise and obligation on the part of the Catholic party. Both parties are sincere and I am happy to witness their marriage.

_____	_____
DATE	PRIEST/DEACON
	_____
	CHURCH
	_____
	CITY & STATE

Petition for Dispensation from the Canonical Form of Marriage

When a Catholic person asks to be married outside of a Catholic church building and in the presence of someone other than a Catholic priest, a form similar to the one that follows is completed by a priest who sends it on to your bishop. This permission is granted for different reasons in different places; ask your priest for the particulars.

With this permission, a marriage contracted outside of a Catholic church is sacramental; without this permission, the church will not recognize your marriage.

Yes, you're quite correct that this is all very confusing. Your priest will be happy to fill in the blanks.

Petition for Dispensation from the Canonical Form of Marriage

To be completed by Priest/Deacon and sent to the Marriage Department of the Diocesan Pastoral Center along with Prenuptial Interview.

_____, the Catholic party, who wishes to marry _____, the non-Catholic party, on _____, requests a dispensation from the Canonical Form of Marriage (C. 1108) so that the marriage can take place in _____

_____

CHURCH, ADDRESS, CITY, STATE

in the presence of _____

NAME AND DENOMINATION

The reason for this request is _____

_____   _____

DATE   PRIEST/DEACON

_____

CHURCH

_____

CITY & STATE

Most Frequently Asked Questions and Their Answers

QUESTION: What about marriages between two Christians of different denominations—a Catholic and a Lutheran, for example. If the wedding is in a Catholic church, can you invite the minister from the Lutheran church to be part of the ceremony?

Usually, yes. Most priests are quite good about inviting the participation of another minister. Some will invite the visitor to say a prayer, pronounce a blessing, read from scripture, or preach the homily. Much will depend on the custom in your town.

QUESTION: Can a Catholic be married in a non-Catholic church?

Sometimes. If, for example, a Catholic man wants to marry a non-Catholic woman and promises to baptize and raise the children as Catholics, it is possible that the wedding ceremony can take place in her church with her minister presiding and witnessing the vows. The technical term for this is *dispensation from form,* and it means that the traditional Catholic ceremony can sometimes be replaced by a ceremony of another sort. This dispensation or permission must come from your bishop, but the request is made through your pastor. Visit with him if you have questions and he'll tell you what is possible in your area.

QUESTION: What if a Catholic person who has never married wants to marry a Lutheran who was married to another Lutheran in a Lutheran church?

Always presume that a marriage entered into by two Protestant people is a valid bond. For a more complete answer in this and any similar instance, call your pastor or the marriage tribunal, which usually has an office in the chancery or bishop's office.

QUESTION: What happens if I disregard the church's laws about marriage or remarriage?

If your marriage is not recognized by the church, you are still bound to worship as a Catholic person, but cannot receive the sacraments. You are not excommunicated but are in an irregular situation. A priest can explain to you how you can explore or begin the process of reconciling with the church.

QUESTION: What about having our wedding day during Lent?

This is generally not a good idea. Lent is a time of penance and preparation for Easter. The festivity of a wedding feast is usually thought to be inappropriate to the season.

QUESTION: Is it a good idea to chew gum during the wedding as a way to keep down the anxiety level?

No!

PART III
Beyond the Footlights

NOTE: *These pages can be duplicated and distributed to members of your wedding party.)*

COPY AND CARRY

The Best Man's Duties

BEFORE THE CEREMONY

- Be certain that at all prewedding festivities there is a driver available who has refrained from alcohol and all other debilitating substances.
- Run interference for the groom so that he does not find himself in any situation that might hinder him in his ability to function on the wedding day.
- If you are entrusted with the rings, see that they arrive at the church when you do and are safely kept in your pants' pocket until they are called for. (Take them out of the jeweler's box first.) Don't wear the rings on your own fingers; they are too easily lost or stuck.
- Get the offering for the priest from the groom and keep it in your jacket pocket.

DURING THE REHEARSAL

- Help get everyone involved into position so that the rehearsal can begin at the appointed hour.
- Find out when and where you will be expected to sign the marriage license.

DURING THE CEREMONY

- Be attentive to the priest in the event that he calls expectedly or unexpectedly for your assistance.
- Be solicitous to the groom in the hour of his great nervousness.

AFTER THE CEREMONY

- Be available at the requested moment to sign the marriage license.
- Thank the priest for his kindness (even if you weren't moved by any particular display of feeling) and offer him the envelope that you were given before the games began. When handing him the envelope, you might say, "Bunny and Claude want you to have this." Do not say, "Here's a little something for your trouble."
- Go to the reception and worry about having to propose the first toast that you have written or borrowed in advance and that you have already practiced several times. If you're not feeling creative, you can borrow this one: "To Ralph and Wanda: may they live long and prosper!"

The Maid or Matron of Honor's Duties

BEFORE THE CEREMONY

- Be certain that at all prewedding festivities there is a driver available who has refrained from alcohol and all other debilitating substances.
- Assist the bride in any situations that may hinder her from getting to the church on time.

AT THE REHEARSAL

- Work with the best man to see that all who have a part in the action are ready at the appointed time in the proper place.
- Ask if, when, and where you are going to sign the marriage license.

DURING THE CEREMONY

- Be attentive to the bride. Be sure you know where the Kleenex is.

AFTER THE CEREMONY

- Be ready to sign the marriage license as requested.
- Proceed with all appropriate haste to the next appointed place.

The Reader's Duties

AT THE REHEARSAL

- Practice, using the microphone, the scripture readings that you have already read at home so often that they are almost memorized.
- Reconcile yourself to the translation of the scripture that has been established for use. Don't ad-lib a new translation, because you will most probably end up with mismatched subjects and verbs.
- Note that the translation in this book is the same as you will find at the church. Ask for a copy of these readings with which to practice, rather than using your own Bible or any other source.
- Make sure you know where you will sit during the ceremony and what your cue is to begin reading.
- Ask whether you will carry the book in the entrance procession or find it already at the pulpit.

BEFORE THE CEREMONY

- Check to see that the book and microphone and your appointed chair are where you were told at the rehearsal to expect them. If it seems that the microphone has not been turned on, ask the priest.
- Make sure that the reading glasses you brought are yours and not Clarence's or Betty's.

DURING THE CEREMONY

- Watch for the cue you have been given and read with relish at the appointed moment.
- Do not say, "The first reading is a reading from...," but announce very simply what the lectionary provides by way of introduction, "A reading from the Book of...."
- When you have concluded, pause and then look at the assembly as you say, "The Word of the Lord."

AFTER THE CEREMONY

- Accept compliments with gracious thanks.

The Ushers' Duties

AT THE REHEARSAL

- Arrive on time and be attentive to the requests and directions of the priest, bride, groom, and mother of the bride.
- Ask where family members will be seated for the ceremony.
- Find the telephone that will be available for emergency use before or during the ceremony. Turn off your own cell phone and remind others to do so.

BEFORE THE CEREMONY

- Be at the church no less than forty-five minutes before the ceremony (unless parish policy calls for a different timetable) dressed and ready to go.
- Use the bathroom now because you'll be too busy even to think about it for quite some time.
- Be ready to assist the priest in moving sanctuary furniture or placing plants and candles.
- See that the aisle runner is securely placed at the head of the aisle and is ready to be unrolled.
- Invite the guests already seated in the back pews to come closer: "Friend, come higher! It's a large church [they're all large churches, even the small ones]; you'll see and hear better closer up. Will you follow me, please?"
- Offer your arm to female guests, who are followed by male guests, and lead them to their seats. Place your hand

on the designated pew, step to one side, and allow them to be seated. Female ushers do not offer their arm, but walk beside the female guests.

- Assume that all guests are friends of both the bride and groom; divide the guests evenly between the sides of the church unless you are told differently.
- After the aisle seats are filled, seat the guests by the side aisles. And use your head: If the church has fifty pews on each side but only one hundred and twenty guests are expected, direct the guests to pews near the front.
- Note that the left side (where there might be a statue of Mary) as you enter is the bride's side where her family will sit. The right side (where there may be a statue of St. Joseph) is the groom's side.
- Seat the grandparents of the groom, the grandparents of the bride, the parents of the groom (if they are not in the procession), and lastly, the mother of the bride (if she is not in the procession). Remember, the groom's family sits facing the male statue; the bride's family sits facing the statue of Mary.
- Ask late-arriving guests to wait in the vestibule until the procession has reached the sanctuary. Remove the guest book, if it has been placed in the vestibule, so that late arrivers can be seated without forming a line at the book. See that the book is given to its attendant, who will request at the reception signatures of those who may not have signed already.
- Roll the carpet down the aisle, checking to see that no major wrinkles will impede the procession. If there is a tube or rope that needs to be ditched, don't put it in the traffic pattern.

- After the procession, seat the latecomers by the side aisles.

DURING THE CEREMONY

- Do not desert the church at any time during the ceremony. If the priest asks for help or to have the windows opened, respond quickly.
- If any guest needs a phone, show him or her where you discovered it to be during the rehearsal.
- If the runner wrinkles or bunches up, straighten it.
- Unless called into service, sit near the back of the church where you can see and be seen.

AFTER THE CEREMONY

- If the bride wants to keep the plastic runner for covering her tomato plants, save it in the place she specified. If it is disposable, dispose of it. If it is to be returned to the rental shop, put it in the car trunk of whosoever will return it later.
- Dispose of all flower boxes, garment bags, and miscellaneous trash.
- Be available to move sanctuary furniture and plants to their permanent homes.
- Sweep up and dispose of rice that may have been thrown.
- Check with the priest to see that all details have been attended to.
- Straighten your tie, breathe a sigh of relief over an important job well done, and proceed to the reception.

Guidelines for Wedding Photographers

A wedding is a religious event. In keeping with the dignity of the sacrament and with reverence for the house of the church in which the marriage takes place, the following guidelines are proposed:

1. The church is not a studio. Photographers are not to move sanctuary furniture (for example, the altar, pulpit, or presider's chair).
2. There should be no disruption or disturbance of the ceremony by the photographer. Use of flash during the ceremony is forbidden.
3. Photographs taken from the back of the church or the balcony are acceptable. They may be taken, without flash, at any time during the ceremony.
4. Use of church facilities is permitted one hour and fifty minutes before the ceremony. The final twenty minutes of this period, at a minimum, are to be left for the bride and groom as a quiet time before the ceremony. The photographer has ninety minutes before the ceremony and may use the church up to one hour after the receiving line has ended.

Parish or diocesan policies take precedence over these guidelines.

These guidelines are adapted from those of the St. Cloud Deanery in the Diocese of St. Cloud in Minnesota.

The Payment Equation Worksheet

What size gift to give to the church for getting you to the altar? Not too difficult. Use one of the following examples to compute your gift.

A Modest Gift:
(Cost of groom's wedding outfit)
+ (cost of cake)
divided by 2
= gift to church ($_____)

A Generous Gift:
(Cost of bride's wedding clothes)
+ (cost of photography)
divided by 2
= gift to church ($_____)

Sample Programs

Sample Program One

THE WEDDING CELEBRATION
Kathleen Marie Kuyava and John Howard Lofstuen
St. Michael's Church

Processional	"Trumpet Voluntary," Purcell
Opening Prayer	
Old Testament Reading	Genesis 2:18–24
Responsorial Psalm	Worship, #36, Psalm 33, "Taste and see the goodness of the Lord"
New Testament Reading	1 John 4:7–12
Gospel	John 15:9–12
Homily	
Exchange of Vows	
Blessing and Exchange of Rings	
Vocal Solo	"One Hand, One Heart"
"Holy, Holy, Holy"	Worship, #253
Memorial Acclamation	#254
Great Amen	#255
The Lord's Prayer	
Nuptial Blessing	
Communion Song	"Lights of the City"
Final Blessing	
Recessional	"Wedding March," Mendelssohn

Parents of the Bride	*Anne and Gene Kuyava*
Parents of the Groom	*Janet and John Lofstuen*
Maid of Honor	*Julie Ann Meyer*
Best Man	*David Mount*
Bridesmaids	*Kim Gaida*
	Jennie Wabrowetz
	Linda Ramsey
	Linda Barnstorf
Groomsmen	*Bill Kirsh*
	Bob Kuyava
	Mark Kuyava
	Wayne Gatlin
Ushers	*Greg Kuyava*
	Keith Swanson
	Steve Wabrowetz
Presider	*Father William Graham*
Reader	*Patrick Murray*
Servers	*Tommy Ernst*
	Kevin Ernst
Organist	*Marie Rock*
Soloist	*Barbara Storms*
Personal Attendants	*Judy Larson*
	Katie Chesness

Sample Program Two

THE WEDDING CELEBRATION
Donna Lou Hardesty and Steven Robert Peterson
St. Michael's Church

Prelude	Soloist
Processional	"Trumpet Voluntary," Purcell
Opening Prayer	
Old Testament Reading	Genesis 2:18–24
Responsorial Psalm	Psalm 33, Worship Hymnal, No. 36
New Testament Reading	1 John 4:7–12
Gospel	John 15:9–12
Homily	
Exchange of Vows	
Blessing and Exchange of Rings	
Hymn	Worship Hymnal, No. 588, "Love Divine, All Loves Excelling"
Nuptial Blessing	
Final Blessing	
Recessional	"Wedding March," Mendelssohn

Parents of the Bride	*Bill Hardesty*
	Karen and Dick Raun
Parents of the Groom	*Doris and Bob Peterson*
Maid of Honor	*Becky Richardson*
Best Man	*Tom Leider*
Bridesmaids	*Sarah Leischke*
	Janet Wiedermann

Groomsmen	*Tom Kuberra*
	Mike Kuberra
Ushers	*Mike Peterson*
	Craig Peterson
Presider	*Father William Graham*
Reader	*Anne Kuyava*
Organist	*Marie Rock*
Soloist	*Julie Adams*
Personal Attendant	*Sheri Johnson*

Rite of Catholic Marriage Within Mass

Prior to the ceremony: music

Parents are seated

Processional: _____

When the bridal party has entered the sanctuary, HYMN:

_____

Greeting, welcome, opening prayer.

Old Testament Reading: _____

Psalm (sung by congregation or soloist): _____

New Testament Reading: _____

Gospel: _____

Homily

Exchange of vows, blessing, and exchange of rings.

Hymn or solo: _____

Acclamations during the eucharistic prayer:

Holy, Holy: _____

Memorial Acclamations: _____

Great Amen: _____

Lord's Prayer, recited or sung by entire congregation.

Nuptial Blessing _____

Blessing and dismissal of congregation.

Recessional: _____

Rite of Catholic Marriage Outside of Mass

Prior to the ceremony: Music (if desired)

Parents are seated

Processional: _____

When bridal party has entered the sanctuary, HYMN: _____
_____

Greeting, welcome, opening prayer.

Old Testament reading: _____

Psalm (sung by congregation or soloist): _____

Second Reading: _____

Gospel: _____

Homily

Exchange of vows, blessing, and exchange of rings.

Hymn or solo: _____

Lord's Prayer, recited or sung by entire congregation.

Nuptial Blessing: _____

Blessing and dismissal of congregation.

Recessional: _____